T0012784

Garfield
FAT CAT 3-PACK
VOLUME 3

BY
JIM DAVIS

BALLANTINE BOOKS • NEW YORK

2007 Ballantine Books Trade Paperback Edition

Copyright © 2007 by PAWS, Inc. All Rights Reserved.
GARFIELD SITS AROUND THE HOUSE: © 1983, 2004 by PAWS, Inc. All Rights Reserved.
"GARFIELD" and the GARFIELD characters are registered and unregistered trademarks of PAWS, Inc.
GARFIELD TIPS THE SCALES: © 1984, 2004 by PAWS, Inc. All Rights Reserved.
"GARFIELD" and the GARFIELD characters are registered and unregistered trademarks of PAWS, Inc.
GARFIELD LOSES HIS FEET: © 1984, 2004 by PAWS, Inc. All Rights Reserved.
"GARFIELD" and the GARFIELD characters are registered and unregistered trademarks of PAWS, Inc.
Based on the Garfield® characters created by Jim Davis.

Published in the United States by Ballantine Books, an imprint of Random House, a division of
Penguin Random House LLC, New York.

BALLANTINE and the HOUSE colophon are registered trademarks of Penguin Random House LLC.

NICKELODEON is a Trademark of Viacom International Inc.

ISBN: 978-0-345-48088-0

Printed in China

randomhousebooks.com

First Colorized Edition: October 2007

19 18 17

Garfield
sits around the house

BY JIM DAVIS

Ballantine Books • New York

A GARFIELD NIGHT...

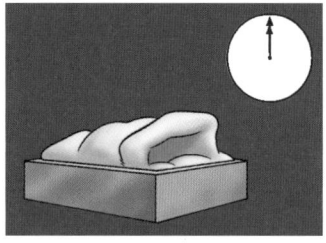

MIDNIGHT SNACK

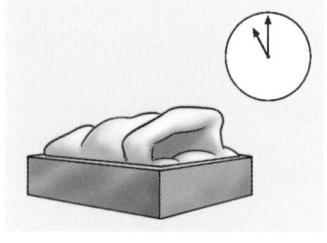

BREAKFAST

JIM DAVIS
1-11

GARFIELD! WHAT HAPPENED!
QUICK! GET THE LICENSE NUMBER OF THAT DOG!
© 1982 PAWS, INC. All Rights Reserved.

JIM DAVIS
1-12

ANY SUDDEN MOVES TOWARD MY FOOD BOWL CAN GET YOU INTO A HEAP OF TROUBLE, BOY
© 1982 PAWS, INC. All Rights Reserved.

1-13
JIM DAVIS

WHAT THE...?
RIBBIT
© 1982 PAWS, INC. All Rights Reserved.

CHOOSE YOUR WEAPON, ODIE
1-14
JIM DAVIS

WE SHALL NOW DUEL WITH NEWSPAPERS

AT ONE PACE!
WHAP!
© 1982 PAWS, INC. All Rights Reserved.

NEAR MISS
1-15
JIM DAVIS

NEAR MISS

DIRECT HIT
© 1982 PAWS, INC. All Rights Reserved.

OKAY, ODIE, YOU HAVE YOUR ROLLED UP NEWSPAPER. I HAVE MINE. LET'S HAVE AT IT!
1-16
JIM DAVIS

WHAP!

WEEKEND EDITION
© 1982 PAWS, INC. All Rights Reserved.

GARFIELD®

BARK!
SPLAT!
JIM DAVIS
1-17

I REALLY ENVY YOU, ODIE
© 1982 PAWS, INC. All Rights Reserved.

POW

IMAGINE... THE FIRST HOUSE PET ON THE MOON

JIM DAVIS
1-18

GOOD MORNING...

...GARFIELD
CAFFEINE MAKES ME NERVOUS
© 1982 PAWS, INC. All Rights Reserved.

© 1982 PAWS, INC. All Rights Reserved.

ODIE! DOGS CAN'T CLIMB TREES!

IT'S AMAZING WHAT ONE CAN ACCOMPLISH WHEN ONE DOESN'T KNOW WHAT ONE CAN'T DO
JIM DAVIS
1-19

HOW ARE YOU BOYS GOING TO GET OUT OF THE TREE?

I DON'T KNOW HOW I'M GETTING OUT OF THE TREE
© 1982 PAWS, INC. All Rights Reserved.
1-20

AS FOR ODIE...
JIM DAVIS

HEY, GARFIELD, HOW ARE YOU GOING TO GET OUT OF THAT TREE?
1-21
JIM DAVIS

BOING!
BOING!

WHY, BY USING MY HEAD... AND JON'S, AND ODIE'S
© 1982 PAWS, INC. All Rights Reserved.

LOOK, GARFIELD, A ROBIN'S NEST. YOU CAN TELL BY THE EGGS
THAT'S NOTHING
JIM DAVIS

LOOK OVER HERE
© 1982 PAWS, INC. All Rights Reserved.

A COW'S NEST
1-22

OH-OH. I GOT A NIBBLE!
JIM DAVIS

DARN, JERKED TOO HARD AGAIN
© 1982 PAWS, INC. All Rights Reserved.
1-23

GARFIELD®

HERE I AM IN THE LAND OF LARGE BREAKFASTS

THIS GIANT PANCAKE SURE TASTES GOOD

WHAT A NICE DREAM
JIM DAVIS
1-24

WHERE'S MY BLANKET?
© 1982 PAWS, INC. All Rights Reserved.

GRANDMA, THIS IS MY CAT, GARFIELD
WELL I'LL BE! HEAVENS TO BETSY! LAND O' GOSHEN!
1-25
JIM DAVIS

I REMEMBER BACK WHEN ALL WE HAD WERE WOOD-BURNING CATS
© 1982 PAWS, INC. All Rights Reserved.

WHAT WON'T THEY THINK OF NEXT?!
BIZARRE

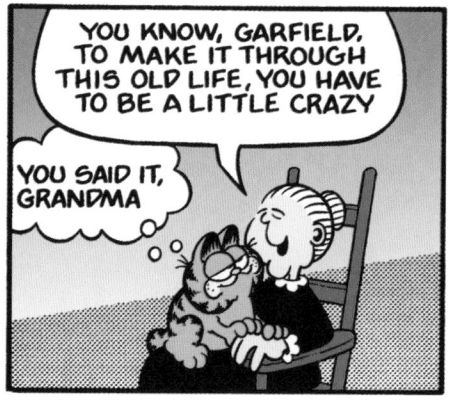
YOU KNOW, GARFIELD, TO MAKE IT THROUGH THIS OLD LIFE, YOU HAVE TO BE A LITTLE CRAZY
YOU SAID IT, GRANDMA

WHY, JUST LOOK AT ME
1-26

© 1982 PAWS, INC. All Rights Reserved.
JIM DAVIS
I TALK TO CATS

HELLO, GARFIELD
JIM DAVIS
1-27

OUT OF THE WAY, DOG!
© 1982 PAWS, INC. All Rights Reserved.

I THINK I LOVE YOU

© 1982 PAWS, INC. All Rights Reserved.

© 1982 PAWS, INC. All Rights Reserved.

© 1982 PAWS, INC. All Rights Reserved.

GARFIELD®

RRRR

GARFIELD! LUNCH TIME!
JIM DAVIS
1-31

GARFIELD! WHERE ARE YOU?

SCREEE

IT IS TIME FOR YOU TO EAT, YOUR MAJESTY
IF I MUST
GARFIELD
© 1982 PAWS, INC. All Rights Reserved.

© 1982 PAWS, INC. All Rights Reserved.

© 1982 PAWS, INC. All Rights Reserved.

© 1982 PAWS, INC. All Rights Reserved.

A BANANA HAS TWO USES
JIM DAVIS
2-4

FOOD...
© 1982 PAWS, INC. All Rights Reserved.

AND ENTERTAINMENT

LOOK AT THAT BEAUTIFUL RAINBOW, GARFIELD
JIM DAVIS 2-5

JUST THINK. AT THE END OF EACH RAINBOW IS A POT OF GOLD

© 1982 PAWS, INC. All Rights Reserved.
THERE'S NOTHING LIKE A HEALTHY RESPECT FOR MOTHER NATURE LACED WITH A LITTLE GREED

JIM DAVIS
2-6

I LIKE YOU, ODIE

IN THE CATNIP AGAIN, GARFIELD?
© 1982 PAWS, INC. All Rights Reserved.

© 1982 PAWS, INC. All Rights Reserved.

EAT THAT OR ELSE, GARFIELD
GARFIELD
JIM DAVIS
2-8

I THINK I'LL...
GARFIELD

ELSE
© 1982 PAWS, INC. All Rights Reserved.

JIM DAVIS
2-9

© 1982 PAWS, INC. All Rights Reserved.

JIM DAVIS
2-10
BE CAREFUL!

WE'LL ALL BE KILLED!
© 1982 PAWS, INC. All Rights Reserved.

I HAVEN'T STARTED THE CAR YET, GARFIELD
THAT'S IT! LET ME OUT

© 1982 PAWS, INC. All Rights Reserved.

© 1982 PAWS, INC. All Rights Reserved.

© 1982 PAWS, INC. All Rights Reserved.

© 1982 PAWS, INC. All Rights Reserved.

JIM DAVIS
2-15

© 1982 PAWS, INC. All Rights Reserved.

WE MUST DO SOMETHING ABOUT YOUR BREATH, GARFIELD
IT'S NOT MY FAULT YOU LEFT THE GARLIC CHEESE OUT LAST NIGHT

RATHER THAN FIX YOUR BREAKFAST EVERY DAY, GARFIELD, I'VE DECIDED TO LET YOU SERVE YOURSELF
CAT CHOW
JIM DAVIS
2-16

CAT CHOW

MAYBE THAT WASN'T SUCH A GOOD IDEA
© 1982 PAWS, INC. All Rights Reserved.

I DON'T BELIEVE I ATE THAT WHOLE BAG OF CAT FOOD
JIM DAVIS
2-17

I'D BETTER JOG SOME OF THIS TUMMY OFF

© 1982 PAWS, INC. All Rights Reserved.

I REALLY DON'T LIKE MYSELF WHEN I'M THIS FAT
JIM DAVIS
2-18

SWIPE!

I CAN'T EVEN ENJOY THE SIMPLE PLEASURES IN LIFE
© 1982 PAWS, INC. All Rights Reserved.

SIT UP, GARFIELD. SIT UP
JIM DAVIS
2-19

SAD
© 1982 PAWS, INC. All Rights Reserved.

OBOY! MY FEET CAN TOUCH THE FLOOR AGAIN!
GARFIELD
JIM DAVIS
2-20

GARFIELD
© 1982 PAWS, INC. All Rights Reserved.

GARFIELD, GARFIELD, GARFIELD
GARFIELD

© 1982 PAWS, INC. All Rights Reserved.

JIM DAVIS

I HATE MONDAYS
© 1982 PAWS, INC. All Rights Reserved.
2-22

JIM DAVIS
2-23

© 1982 PAWS, INC. All Rights Reserved.

JUST STAYING IN SHAPE IN CASE I EVER GET THAT HUNGRY

WHAT TIME IS IT, GARFIELD?
JIM DAVIS
2-24

© 1982 PAWS, INC. All Rights Reserved.

WHAT AM I DOING? I CAN'T TELL TIME

Dear Garfield,
My dog chases my cat all over the house. How can I make them get along?
2-25
JIM DAVIS

THERE'S ONLY ONE SURE WAY TO IMPROVE THEIR RELATIONSHIP

SHOOT THE DOG
© 1982 PAWS, INC. All Rights Reserved.

JIM DAVIS

OKAY, GARFIELD. ONE BITE

© 1982 PAWS, INC. All Rights Reserved.
2-26

COUGH COUGH
JIM DAVIS
2-27

GASP!

OKAY, NO MORE DRY CAT FOOD
© 1982 PAWS, INC. All Rights Reserved.

© 1982 PAWS, INC. All Rights Reserved.

JIM DAVIS 3-1
DINNER IS READY, GARFIELD

I MOVED THE TABLE OVER HERE
© 1982 PAWS, INC. All Rights Reserved.

CRUNCH
JIM DAVIS
3-2

CRUNCH
CRUNCH
CRUNCH

THAT FROZEN PIZZA WOULD BE MUCH BETTER IF YOU BAKED IT FIRST
© 1982 PAWS, INC. All Rights Reserved.

HERE, ODIE
JIM DAVIS
3-3

I GOT YOU A RUBBER BONE
© 1982 PAWS, INC. All Rights Reserved.

JIM DAVIS 3-4

© 1982 PAWS, INC. All Rights Reserved.

SMACK!
SLURP!
JIM DAVIS
3-5

YOU HAVE THE MANNERS OF A PIG, GARFIELD. SLOW DOWN AND SPIT OUT THE SEEDS

RATA TATA
TATA TATA
© 1982 PAWS, INC. All Rights Reserved.

JIM DAVIS
3-6

© 1982 PAWS, INC. All Rights Reserved.

GARFIELD®

WHAT DO YOU THINK, GARFIELD?
DON'T ASK

THERE'S NOTHING LIKE CAMPING OUT IN COLD WEATHER
THAT'S FOR SURE
JIM DAVIS
3-7

AS THE TEMPERATURE DROPS, THE CIRCULATION GETS GOING
AND THE FEET GET NUMB
© 1982 PAWS, INC. All Rights Reserved.

THIS IS NATURE AT HER BEST!
I'D SETTLE FOR LESS

WE HAVE EVERYTHING... OUR FIRE, OUR SHELTER...

OUR COFFEE ON A STICK

WHAT A DISMAL DAY. I THINK I'LL STAY IN BED ALL DAY
JIM DAVIS
3-8

GOOD MORNING, GARFIELD. IT'S A BEAUTIFUL DAY TODAY

WHAT A BEAUTIFUL DAY. I THINK I'LL STAY IN BED ALL DAY
© 1982 PAWS, INC. All Rights Reserved.

HEY, GARFIELD, YOU KNOW THE DOG NEXT DOOR?
WHAT A LOSER. A REAL JERK. I HATE HIM
JIM DAVIS
3-9

HE MOVED AWAY YESTERDAY

A PRINCE OF A DOG. I'LL MISS HIM. THE NEIGHBORHOOD WON'T BE THE SAME WITHOUT HIM
© 1982 PAWS, INC. All Rights Reserved.

JIM DAVIS

AHCHOO!
© 1982 PAWS, INC. All Rights Reserved.
3-10

GESUNDHEIT
SNIFF

AND NOW, A WORD FROM OUR SPONSOR
JIM DAVIS
3-11

ZOOM
© 1982 PAWS, INC. All Rights Reserved.

WELCOME BACK

OKAY, ODIE, YOU PUSH THE CAKE OFF AND I'LL CATCH IT
JIM DAVIS

DON'T TIP IT! DON'T TIP IT!
© 1982 PAWS, INC. All Rights Reserved.
3-12

YOU TIPPED IT

JIM DAVIS
3-13

PUNT

HAVE YOU KICKED YOUR DOG TODAY?
© 1982 PAWS, INC. All Rights Reserved.

Garfield®

HEY, GARFIELD. MY PICTURES JUST CAME IN
WHOOPTY-DOO

I LOVE PICTURES
PAPER MEMORIES OF PLASTIC PEOPLE

WHAT'S THIS?

YOU'VE BEEN PLAYING WITH MY CAMERA AGAIN, HAVEN'T YOU, GARFIELD?
WHO ME? THE LEONARDO DA VINCI OF THE SHUTTERBUG SET?
JIM DAVIS
3-14 © 1982 PAWS, INC. All Rights Reserved.

© 1982 PAWS, INC. All Rights Reserved.

© 1982 PAWS, INC. All Rights Reserved.

© 1982 PAWS, INC. All Rights Reserved.

© 1982 PAWS, INC. All Rights Reserved.

© 1982 PAWS, INC. All Rights Reserved.

Garfield®
LAST ONE IN'S A ROTTEN EGG!
YOU FIRST, POOKY
BACK FLIP!
© 1982 PAWS, INC. All Rights Reserved.
3-21
JIM DAVIS

ROWR
JIM DAVIS
3-22

BOOT
© 1982 PAWS, INC. All Rights Reserved.

AND NOW FOR THE MAIN ATTRACTION

TESTING, ONE, TWO. TESTING, ONE, TWO
ROWR
3-23

CAN YOU HEAR ME THERE IN THE BACK?
© 1982 PAWS, INC. All Rights Reserved.

GOOD
JIM DAVIS

I LOVE SHOW BUSINESS. GIMME THE FULL MOON. GIMME THE FENCE
3-24

KAWHOCK!
© 1982 PAWS, INC. All Rights Reserved.

GIMME THE BROKEN TEETH. GIMME THE MULTIPLE LACERATIONS
JIM DAVIS

© 1982 PAWS, INC. All Rights Reserved.

© 1982 PAWS, INC. All Rights Reserved.

GARFIELD®
CHOMP!
SLURP! GULP!
Z
STAY OUT OF MY DREAMS
JIM DAVIS
3-28
© 1982 PAWS, INC. All Rights Reserved.

JIM DAVIS 3-29

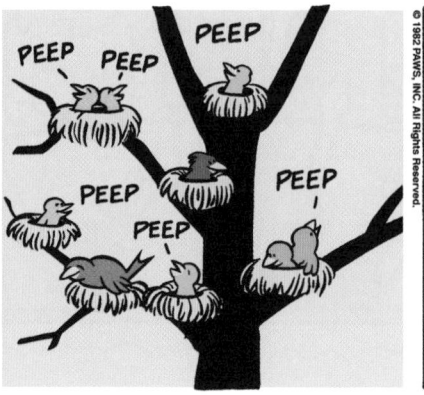
PEEP
PEEP
PEEP
PEEP
PEEP
PEEP

IT LOOKS LIKE THERE WILL BE A BUMPER CROP OF CAT FOOD THIS YEAR
© 1982 PAWS, INC. All Rights Reserved.

JIM DAVIS
3-30

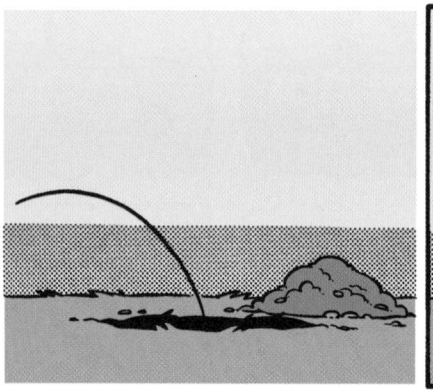

I WISH ODIE WOULD FINISH WHAT HE STARTS
© 1982 PAWS, INC. All Rights Reserved.

JIM DAVIS
3-31

BONE BREATH!
© 1982 PAWS, INC. All Rights Reserved.

4-1
JIM DAVIS

© 1982 PAWS, INC. All Rights Reserved.

TOO MUCH ROPE

JIM DAVIS
4-2

DON'T YOU DARE WALK ACROSS THE TABLE WITH THOSE MUDDY FEET

© 1982 PAWS, INC. All Rights Reserved.

JIM DAVIS
4-3

© 1982 PAWS, INC. All Rights Reserved.

I MUST HAVE BLOWN A FUSE

© 1982 PAWS, INC. All Rights Reserved.

JIM DAVIS
4-5

IT LOOKS AS THOUGH I'M ON ANOTHER DIET
© 1982 PAWS, INC. All Rights Reserved.

RRRRRR
JIM DAVIS 4-6

ROWR!

NOT GOOD
© 1982 PAWS, INC. All Rights Reserved.

WHEN I DIET, I GET MEAN
JIM DAVIS
4-7

WHEN I DIET, I ALSO GET WEAK
© 1982 PAWS, INC. All Rights Reserved.

OH,NO! POOKY'S BROKEN A STITCH!
JIM DAVIS
4-8

WAHHH!
© 1982 PAWS, INC. All Rights Reserved.

WHEN I DIET, I GET EMOTIONAL

UH-OH
JIM DAVIS
4-9

© 1982 PAWS, INC. All Rights Reserved.

WHEN I'M OFF THIS DIET, I'M GOING TO EAT LASAGNA, CAKE, ICE CREAM, MASHED POTATOES...
JIM DAVIS
4-10

© 1982 PAWS, INC. All Rights Reserved.

I JUST GAINED TWO POUNDS!

GARFIELD®

FOOM!

BOINK
4-11

BEEP! BEEP!

BZT

JUST AS I THOUGHT. ALL THE WARRANTIES EXPIRED YESTERDAY

© 1982 PAWS, INC. All Rights Reserved.

© 1982 PAWS, INC. All Rights Reserved.

DO YOU KNOW WHAT I LIKE ABOUT WOMEN?
JIM DAVIS
4-15

THEY ARE SO SOFT

COME TO THINK OF IT...
© 1982 PAWS, INC. All Rights Reserved.

PURRR
JIM DAVIS
4-16

PURRR
© 1982 PAWS, INC. All Rights Reserved.

SORRY ABOUT THAT, ARLENE

OKAY, GARFIELD
JIM DAVIS
4-17

I CAUGHT THE MOUSE AND ATE IT

YOU CAN OPEN YOUR EYES NOW
© 1982 PAWS, INC. All Rights Reserved.

GARFIELD®

YOU'RE LUCKY THIS FENCE IS BETWEEN US, DOG

COME ON, PUT 'EM UP

TAKE THAT!
BOP!
JIM DAVIS

HEY, CHICKEN, COME BACK HERE AND FIGHT LIKE A MAN

© 1982 PAWS, INC. All Rights Reserved.
4-18

YOU HAD TO PAINT THE GATE TODAY
SMACK!

© 1982 PAWS, INC. All Rights Reserved.

© 1982 PAWS, INC. All Rights Reserved.

© 1982 PAWS, INC. All Rights Reserved.

WHAT'S THAT?
JIM DAVIS
4-22

THERE MUST BE A LEAK IN THE ROOF

IF IT ISN'T A LEAK IN THE ROOF, I DON'T WANT TO KNOW WHAT IT IS
© 1982 PAWS, INC. All Rights Reserved.

WOULD YOU LIKE A STEAK, ODIE?
© 1982 PAWS, INC. All Rights Reserved.

YOU DIDN'T SAY, "MAY I?"
4-23
JIM DAVIS

HEY, ODIE, HOW ABOUT A FREE TRIP TO LOOSE TOOTH CITY?
4-24

WHIRRRR!

I GOTTA CUT BACK ON MY FOLLOW-THROUGH
© 1982 PAWS, INC. All Rights Reserved.
JIM DAVIS

GARFIELD®

Z

DON'T WORRY, ODIE, OLD BUDDY. I'LL GET YOU DOWN
ORK ORK
© 1982 PAWS, INC. All Rights Reserved.

PTUI
POW!
JIM DAVIS
4-25

CLOSE ENOUGH

© 1982 PAWS, INC. All Rights Reserved.

© 1982 PAWS, INC. All Rights Reserved.

WELCOME TO THE ROCKY OXNARD
JIM DAVIS
4-29

SHOW

YOU KNOW RUSSIAN AUNTIE OFFER. YOU BLAH BLAH AND BLAH BLAH BLAH BLAH
I ALWAYS TURN THE VOLUME KNOB THE WRONG WAY
© 1982 PAWS, INC. All Rights Reserved.

JIM DAVIS
4-30

I GOTTA FIX THAT VERTICAL HOLD
© 1982 PAWS, INC. All Rights Reserved.

WE'LL BE RIGHT BACK AFTER THIS WORD FROM OUR SPONSOR
JIM DAVIS
5-1

SASQUATCH

WELCOME BACK
© 1982 PAWS, INC. All Rights Reserved.

GARFIELD®

I JUST GOT COMFORTABLE, GARFIELD. DO YOU **ABSOLUTELY** HAVE TO BE LET OUT?

OH, YES

VERY WELL, THEN

SUCKER
JIM DAVIS 5-2
© 1982 PAWS, INC. All Rights Reserved.

GUESS WHERE WE'RE GOING, GARFIELD?
TO A HAYSEED CONVENTION?
JIM DAVIS
5-3

YESIREE, WE'RE GONNA SEE MOM AND DAD ON THE FARM. WE'RE GONNA SLOP THE PIGS AND PLUCK THE CHICKENS. BOY HOWDY, WE'RE GONNA HAVE US A TIME

THAT IS, IF YOUR FATHER DOESN'T BEAT THE HECK OUT OF YOU FOR DOING THAT STUPID STEREOTYPE
© 1982 PAWS, INC. All Rights Reserved.

MOM!
JIM DAVIS
5-4

© 1982 PAWS, INC. All Rights Reserved.
SON!

SON?
MOM?

HOW HAVE YOU BEEN, MOM?
NEVER MIND THAT

JIM DAVIS
5-5
HERE, EAT, EAT, EAT

© 1982 PAWS, INC. All Rights Reserved.
YOU'RE MY KIND OF WOMAN

© 1982 PAWS, INC. All Rights Reserved.

© 1982 PAWS, INC. All Rights Reserved.

© 1982 PAWS, INC. All Rights Reserved.

GARFIELD®

SCREEEE
CRUNCH!

YABBA!
YABBA!
YABBA!

SOCK!

HUMAN BEINGS...WHY DO THEY YELL AT EACH OTHER? WHY DO THEY HURT EACH OTHER?
JIM DAVIS
5-9
© 1982 PAWS, INC. All Rights Reserved.

URF

WHAT DO YOU KNOW?
WOING!

JUST WHAT IS A MONDAY?
GARFIELD
JIM DAVIS 5-10

PLIP
GARFIELD
© 1982 PAWS, INC. All Rights Reserved.

MONDAY IS A DAY DESIGNED TO ADD DEPRESSION TO AN OTHERWISE HAPPY WEEK

JUST WHAT IS LIFE? LIFE IS A LOT LIKE A HOT BATH
JIM DAVIS
5-11

IT FEELS GOOD WHILE YOU'RE IN IT

BUT THE LONGER YOU STAY... THE MORE WRINKLED YOU GET
© 1982 PAWS, INC. All Rights Reserved.

JUST WHAT IS TELEVISION?
JIM DAVIS
5-12

TELEVISION NOT ONLY GIVES THE EYEBALLS SOMETHING TO DO,
© 1982 PAWS, INC. All Rights Reserved.

BUT IT'S A SOCIALLY ACCEPTABLE EXCUSE TO SNACK

JUST WHAT IS A GOLDFISH?
JIM DAVIS
5-13

A GOLDFISH IS AN AQUATIC EXPRESSION OF BEAUTY AND GRACE THAT PROVIDES ITS OBSERVERS WITH MANY HOURS OF BLISSFUL MEDITATION
© 1982 PAWS, INC. All Rights Reserved.

IT ALSO MAKES A DARN FINE BREAKFAST

JUST WHAT IS A DOG?
JIM DAVIS
5-14

LET ME PUT IT THIS WAY...

IF A DOG WERE A FAUCET, IT WOULD LEAK
© 1982 PAWS, INC. All Rights Reserved.

JUST WHAT IS A CAT? A CAT IS A FURRY ANIMAL, COMPLETE WITH DOG NIBBLERS AND FURNITURE SHREDDERS
JIM DAVIS
5-15

HACK!

THE HAIRBALLS IN THE THROAT ARE ALSO STANDARD EQUIPMENT
© 1982 PAWS, INC. All Rights Reserved.

© 1982 PAWS, INC. All Rights Reserved.

© 1982 PAWS, INC. All Rights Reserved.

© 1982 PAWS, INC. All Rights Reserved.

© 1982 PAWS, INC. All Rights Reserved.

© 1982 PAWS, INC. All Rights Reserved.

GARFIELD®
(CLICK) EEEEEEEE!
(CLICK) YOU KNOW, PLEASURE MOTORS
(CLICK)
5-23
(CLICK) HI YUH, KIDS!
PICK A STATION AND STAY WITH IT, GARFIELD
CLICK!
© 1982 PAWS, INC. All Rights Reserved.
JIM DAVIS

5-24
JIM DAVIS

BLUT
BLUT
BLUT
BLUT
BLUT
© 1982 PAWS, INC. All Rights Reserved.

WHEN ARE YOU GOING TO LEARN TO CONTROL THAT TEMPER OF YOURS, GARFIELD?
THE EXACT SAME INSTANT THEY INVENT AN EASY POURING CATSUP

ANY CAT CAN USE A BOTTLE OPENER
JIM DAVIS
5-25

BUT IT TAKES A REAL MAN TO USE HIS TEETH
© 1982 PAWS, INC. All Rights Reserved.

A REAL STUPID MAN

WHAT ARE YOU PLANTING, GARFIELD?
JIM DAVIS
5-26

© 1982 PAWS, INC. All Rights Reserved.

BIRDSEED?

© 1982 PAWS, INC. All Rights Reserved.

© 1982 PAWS, INC. All Rights Reserved.

© 1982 PAWS, INC. All Rights Reserved.

GARFIELD®

SNAP

© 1982 PAWS, INC. All Rights Reserved.

BLAT!
5-30
JIM DAVIS

IS IT WINDY OUT, GARFIELD?
NOT SO YOU'D NOTICE

© 1982 PAWS, INC. All Rights Reserved.

©1982 PAWS, INC. All Rights Reserved.

©1982 PAWS, INC. All Rights Reserved.

LAP
LAP
LAP
JIM DAVIS
6-3

LAP
LAP

©1982 PAWS, INC. All Rights Reserved.

AH
AH
AH
JIM DAVIS
6-4

WAH-
CHOO!

SNIFF
©1982 PAWS, INC. All Rights Reserved.

AH
AH
AH
6-5

WAH-
CHOO!

JIM DAVIS
©1982 PAWS, INC. All Rights Reserved.

GARFIELD®

I LOVE YOU, BUNNY RABBIT

I LOVE YOU, TOO, DEER

I LOVE YOU ALL
JIM DAVIS 6-6

WHAT THE...?
I BROUGHT SOME FRIENDS HOME FOR DINNER
©1982 PAWS, INC. All Rights Reserved.

©1982 PAWS, INC. All Rights Reserved.

©1982 PAWS, INC. All Rights Reserved.

©1982 PAWS, INC. All Rights Reserved.

GOOD! HERE COMES HELP
6-10
JIM DAVIS

© 1982 PAWS, INC. All Rights Reserved.
HANG IN THERE, BABY. HA, HA

I CAN SEE THE HEADLINES: "CAT KILLS JOCULAR PASSER-BY"

I CAN'T BELIEVE I'VE BEEN HANGING IN THIS TREE ALL WEEK
6-11
JIM DAVIS

© 1982 PAWS, INC. All Rights Reserved.
NOW I CAN

JIM DAVIS

GETTING OUT OF THIS TREE WILL BE SIMPLER THAN I THOUGHT

6-12
© 1982 PAWS, INC. All Rights Reserved.

GARFIELD

HAVEN'T WE MET SOMEWHERE BEFORE? PERHAPS A PASTA PLACE IN PALERMO?

WHAT'S THAT? OH NO, MY DEAR. EVEN THOUGH YOU ARE JUST A LASAGNA, I ADMIRE YOU FOR YOUR MIND

YOU KNOW I CAN'T RESIST YOU WHEN YOU WEAR GARLIC SAUCE ON YOUR NOODLES
©1982 PAWS, INC. All Rights Reserved.

THIS COULD BE THE START OF A LONG AND MEANINGFUL RELATIONSHIP

JIM DAVIS

I DESPISE LONG ENGAGEMENTS
6-13

WOW. I'M GOING TO BE FOUR YEARS OLD THIS SATURDAY
JUNE
JIM DAVIS

IT'S TIME TO REFLECT UPON MY ACCOMPLISHMENTS. IT'S TIME TO REMINISCE ABOUT GOOD TIMES...
6-14

IT'S TIME TO LIE ABOUT MY AGE
JUNE
© 1982 PAWS, INC. All Rights Reserved.

FACE IT, GARFIELD, YOU'RE NOT GETTING ANY YOUNGER
JIM DAVIS

I WISH THERE WERE SOMETHING I COULD DO ABOUT THE AGING PROCESS
6-15

I'D DO SIT-UPS, BUT I COULDN'T STAND THE NOISE
© 1982 PAWS, INC. All Rights Reserved.

JIM DAVIS
6-16

© 1982 PAWS, INC. All Rights Reserved.
YAWN

YOU KNOW YOU'RE GETTING OLDER WHEN YOUR FAVORITE LATE NIGHT SHOW IS THE SIX O'CLOCK NEWS

JIM DAVIS

6-17

© 1982 PAWS, INC. All Rights Reserved.

IT HARDLY SEEMS POSSIBLE I'M CELEBRATING MY FOURTH BIRTHDAY TOMORROW
JIM DAVIS
6-18

BARK!
SPLAT!

TIME FLIES WHEN YOU'RE HAVING FUN
© 1982 PAWS, INC. All Rights Reserved.

HAPPY BIRTHDAY, GARFIELD!
JIM DAVIS

GULP!
© 1982 PAWS, INC. All Rights Reserved.

MAYBE YOU SHOULD HAVE BLOWN THE CANDLES OUT FIRST
6-19

©1982 PAWS, INC. All Rights Reserved.

JIM DAVIS
6-21

HELLO. I'M NERMAL, THE WORLD'S CUTEST KITTEN, HERE TO DO CUTE KITTEN THINGS IN ORDER TO CHARM THE PANTS OFF YOUR OWNER AND POINT OUT HOW UNCUTE YOU ARE

I HATE MONDAY
© 1982 PAWS, INC. All Rights Reserved.

GIMME THAT
JIM DAVIS
6-22

I FAIL TO SEE WHAT'S SO CUTE ABOUT YARN

OR KITTENS, FOR THAT MATTER
© 1982 PAWS, INC. All Rights Reserved.

GARFIELD
JIM DAVIS
6-23

GEE, SINCE NERMAL ISN'T HERE, I'LL EAT HIS FOOD, TOO
GARFIELD
© 1982 PAWS, INC. All Rights Reserved.

GARFIELD

OKAY, NERMAL, GO AHEAD AND JUMP
JIM DAVIS 6-24

I'LL HAVE YOU OUT OF THERE IN TWO SHAKES OF A CAT'S TAIL
© 1982 PAWS, INC. All Rights Reserved.

OR IS THAT, TWO SHAKES OF A LAMB'S TAIL?
SPLAT!

COME ON, NERMAL. LET'S FIGHT
JIM DAVIS 6-25

ROWR!

WHAT A REVOLTING DEVELOPMENT THIS IS
© 1982 PAWS, INC. All Rights Reserved.

LET'S HAVE SOME FUN, NERMAL
JIM DAVIS 6-26

I'LL TIE YOU IN NICE AND SAFE

SEE YUH
© 1982 PAWS, INC. All Rights Reserved.

GARFIELD®

SPLUT
GARFIELD

DON'T YOU DARE LAUGH. I HATE IT WHEN SOMEONE HAS A LAUGH AT MY EXPENSE
©1982 PAWS, INC. All Rights Reserved.
JIM DAVIS

SPLAT

IF I LAUGH, GARFIELD WILL KILL ME. IF I DON'T LAUGH, I'LL BURST

WAH HA HA HA!
6-27

HA HA HA, WHEEE

JIM DAVIS

6-28

IT'S TIME YOU GO ON ANOTHER DIET, GARFIELD
© 1982 PAWS, INC. All Rights Reserved.

JUST WHAT IS A DIET?
JIM DAVIS
6-29

A DIET IS TOO LITTLE OF A GOOD THING. A DIET IS MAKING A MOLEHILL OUT OF A MOUNTAIN

A DIET IS THE SUBJECT OF A LOT OF STUPID PLATITUDES
© 1982 PAWS, INC. All Rights Reserved.

I HATE DIETS
JIM DAVIS
6-30

I'D GET OUT OF BED TO HAVE BREAKFAST
© 1982 PAWS, INC. All Rights Reserved.

BUT IT'S NOT WORTH THE TRIP

I'M STRONG. I CAN HANDLE THIS DIET
JIM DAVIS 7-1

SNIFF
© 1982 PAWS, INC. All Rights Reserved.

THEN WHY DO I FEEL LIKE I'VE JUST LOST MY BEST FRIEND?

THAT APPLE IS ALL YOU'RE GETTING FOR DINNER, GARFIELD
JIM DAVIS
7-2

© 1982 PAWS, INC. All Rights Reserved.

GIMME FOOD. LOTS OF IT. AND RIGHT NOW
JIM DAVIS
7-3

YES, SIR
© 1982 PAWS, INC. All Rights Reserved.

TWO ADJECTIVES NEVER USED TO DESCRIBE A CAT ARE: "WISHY" AND "WASHY"

GARFIELD®

THERE MUST BE MORE TO LIFE THAN THIS. I'M GOING TO FIND SOME EXCITEMENT

YUK!

YOU'RE OUT OF YOUR TERRITORY, AREN'T YOU, FELLA?
©1982 PAWS, INC. All Rights Reserved.

HELLO THERE, STRAY CAT
POUND

WHERE HAVE YOU BEEN?
CULTIVATING A HEALTHY DISLIKE FOR EXCITEMENT
JIM DAVIS
7-4

IN OUR FAST-PACED WORLD, RELAXATION IS PRACTICALLY A LOST ART
7-5
JIM DAVIS

Z

PRACTICALLY
© 1982 PAWS, INC. All Rights Reserved.

HERE YOU GO, GARFIELD
TABLE SCRAPS!
GARFIELD
JIM DAVIS
7-6

SPLAT!
GARFIELD

THAT'S DOG FOOD
GARFIELD
© 1982 PAWS, INC. All Rights Reserved.

JIM DAVIS
7-7
AREN'T YOU CUTE

ROWR!

WHY, YOU VICIOUS BRUTE!
WHAT HAPPENED TO "CUTE"?
© 1982 PAWS, INC. All Rights Reserved.

© 1982 PAWS, INC. All Rights Reserved.

GARFIELD®

GARFIELD

GARFIELD

GARFIELD
©1982 PAWS, INC. All Rights Reserved.

TOUCH MY FOOD AND YOU'RE ONE DEAD DOG
GARFIELD
JIM DAVIS
7-11

MY FEAR OF MONDAYS IS REALLY CHILDISH
JIM DAVIS
7-12

I MUST LEARN TO FACE THEM LIKE A MAN

YOU FIRST, POOKY
© 1982 PAWS, INC. All Rights Reserved.

WHAT'S THAT YOU SAY, LITTLE FELLA?
JIM DAVIS
7-13

OH, VERY WELL. I'LL HOLD YOU
© 1982 PAWS, INC. All Rights Reserved.

POOKY NEEDS ME

GOBBLE! SMACK! SLURP!
JIM DAVIS
7-14

GARFIELD!
UH-OH
© 1982 PAWS, INC. All Rights Reserved.

STAY RIGHT WHERE YOU ARE OR THE TEDDY BEAR GETS IT

© 1982 PAWS, INC. All Rights Reserved.

© 1982 PAWS, INC. All Rights Reserved.

GARFIELD®

DID YOU WHISTLE AT MY GIRL?
NO, SIR, I DIDN'T

ROWR!

IT WAS MY CAT! IT WAS MY CAT!
JIM DAVIS

WELL, I HOPE YOU'RE HAPPY
7-18
©1982 PAWS, INC. All Rights Reserved.

IT'S BEEN A LONG TIME SINCE I HEARD A GOOD "SPLUT"
JIM DAVIS
7-19

PUNT

SPLUT
© 1982 PAWS, INC. All Rights Reserved.

BARK!
SPLUT
JIM DAVIS
7-20

BARK!
SPLUT
© 1982 PAWS, INC. All Rights Reserved.

GARFIELD, I WOULDN'T SAY YOU'RE FAT...
GARFIELD
JIM DAVIS

BUT HERMAN MELVILLE WANTS TO WRITE A BOOK ABOUT YOU
GARFIELD
7-21

SPLUT
GARFIELD
© 1982 PAWS, INC. All Rights Reserved.

UH-OH! TOO HARD!
JIM DAVIS

WHY HAVEN'T THOSE EGGS COME DOWN? MAYBE THEY STUCK TO THE CEILING. MAYBE I SHOULD LOOK
7-22

SPLUT
© 1982 PAWS, INC. All Rights Reserved.

SPLUT
SPLUT
JIM DAVIS
7-23

BLAT
BLAT
BLAT
© 1982 PAWS, INC. All Rights Reserved.

SPLUT

NO ONE KNOWS THE TREPIDATION I FEEL KNOWING SOMEWHERE OUT THERE IS A "SPLUT" WITH MY NAME ON IT
JIM DAVIS
7-24

OOP!
© 1982 PAWS, INC. All Rights Reserved.

SPLUT

GARFIELD®

THERE ARE PRIZES AT THE BOTTOM OF THE CAT FOOD
CAT FOOD

BANZAI!
CAT FOOD
JIM DAVIS
7-25

MUNCH MUNCH
CAT FOOD
©1982 PAWS, INC. All Rights Reserved.

MUNCH MUNCH
CAT FOOD

TWEET TWEET
CAT FOOD

TWEET TWEET
CAT FOOD

© 1982 PAWS, INC. All Rights Reserved.

© 1982 PAWS, INC. All Rights Reserved.

© 1982 PAWS, INC. All Rights Reserved.

NIGHTTIME IS MAGIC TO CATS. CATS ARE VERY COMFORTABLE WITH DARKNESS
KLUNK
KLUNK
JIM DAVIS 7-29
© 1982 PAWS, INC. All Rights Reserved.
ESPECIALLY IF THEIR DARN FLASHLIGHTS DON'T WORK

ARRRGH!
© 1982 PAWS, INC. All Rights Reserved.
YOU'RE SUPPOSED TO BE ON MY SIDE!
JIM DAVIS 7-30

WHAT SHOULD I DO THIS WEEKEND?
CLICK!
I THINK I'LL JUST SIT AROUND AND BLINK A LOT
© 1982 PAWS, INC. All Rights Reserved.
JIM DAVIS 7-31

GARFIELD®

YAWN
JIM DAVIS
8-1

GARFIELD
©1982 PAWS, INC. All Rights Reserved.

I HATE TO EAT ALONE
GARFIELD

© 1982 PAWS, INC. All Rights Reserved.

JIM DAVIS
8-5

BARK

I HATE DOGS
© 1982 PAWS, INC. All Rights Reserved.

IT'S DINNER TIME, GARFIELD
8-6
JIM DAVIS

GARFIEEELD
BONG!
BONG!
BONG!

YOU RANG?
© 1982 PAWS, INC. All Rights Reserved.

I WONDER WHAT THIS MACHINE IS
CLICK
JIM DAVIS
8-7

SPLAT
WHIRRRR
ZIP

IT IS OBVIOUSLY SOME SORT OF CAT TORTURE DEVICE
© 1982 PAWS, INC. All Rights Reserved.

GARFIELD®
THIS LOOKS LIKE THE PERFECT SPOT FOR A CLANDESTINE RENDEZVOUS
HERE COMES MY DOUBLE AGENT NOW
EEEAWKEY, 43, AND THE LETTER C
AN INFANT IN YOUR LAP MAY DAMPEN YOUR SPIRITS
UH-OH! IT'S COUNTER INTELLIGENCE!
DOWN IN FRONT, GARFIELD
QUIET, YOU FOOL! YOU COULD BLOW MY COVER!
©1982 PAWS, INC. All Rights Reserved.
8-8 JIM DAVIS

HMMM. A HOLLOW STUMP WITH A THING IN IT... I GOTTA FIND OUT WHAT IT IS
RRRR
JIM DAVIS
8-9

RRRRRRR

TUESDAY
© 1982 PAWS, INC. All Rights Reserved.

EVEN THOUGH "CURIOSITY KILLED THE CAT" IS JUST A SILLY SUPERSTITION, I MUST KNOW WHAT'S IN THIS STUMP
RRRR
JIM DAVIS
8-10

ROAR!
RIP!
CHOMP
SNORT!

HA HA HA, SILLY ME
© 1982 PAWS, INC. All Rights Reserved.

I'M GOING TO GIVE THAT THING IN THE STUMP A TASTE OF THIS ROCK
JIM DAVIS
8-11

MUNCH MUNCH PTOOEY!
© 1982 PAWS, INC. All Rights Reserved.

I DIDN'T KNOW STONES HAD BONES
BURP

ALL RIGHT, WHATEVER YOU ARE, COME OUT OF THERE!
RRRR
JIM DAVIS
8-12

YOU? A MOUSE WAS MAKING ALL THAT NOISE?

THIS STUMP HAS REALLY GREAT ACOUSTICS
© 1982 PAWS, INC. All Rights Reserved.

I CAN'T BELIEVE YOU WERE THE THING IN THE STUMP THAT'S BEEN SCARING ME ALL WEEK
JIM DAVIS
8-13

WHY, I'M GONNA...

DOWN, GUIDO, DOWN
© 1982 PAWS, INC. All Rights Reserved.

I'VE LEARNED MY LESSON. I'M NOT MESSING WITH THINGS IN HOLLOW STUMPS AGAIN
RRRR
JIM DAVIS
8-14

I'M GOING HOME WHERE IT'S SAFE

OH, NO
RRRR
RRR
© 1982 PAWS, INC. All Rights Reserved.

GARFIELD®

SOME DAY I'M GONNA BE THE GREATEST CATERWAULER IN THE WORLD. THEY'RE GONNA CALL ME "CATS WAULER"

ROWR!

CHUKONG!

AROOO

WHOCK!

WHY DO YOU DO IT, GARFIELD?
DUES. I'M JUST PAYING MY DUES
JIM DAVIS
8-15 ©1982 PAWS, INC. All Rights Reserved.

THE SHOCKING TRUTH...REVEALED!!

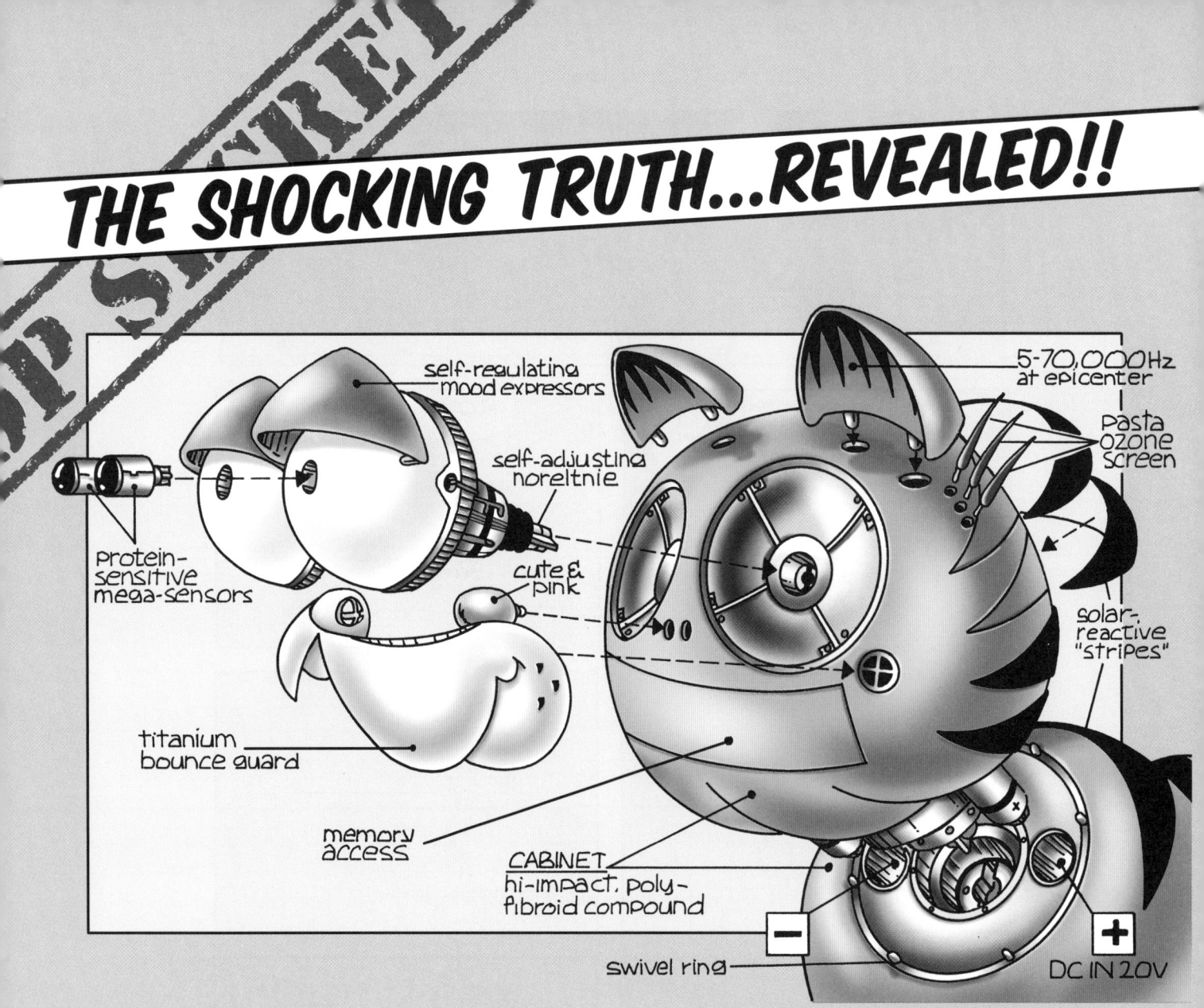

MAJOR COMIC STRIP CHARACTER REPLACED BY A MACHINE!

Rumors are running rampant that Garfield the cat has retired to a South Sea island and has been replaced by a bionic duplicate. This schematic mysteriously ended up in the hands of the publisher. Fact . . . or fiction? Read this book and determine for yourself.

Garfield tips the scales

BY JIM DAVIS

Ballantine Books • New York

CRUNCH CRUNCH CRUNCH
JIM DAVIS
8-16

I KNOW YOU'RE HUNGRY, GARFIELD
CRUNCH CRUNCH
© 1982 PAWS, INC. All Rights Reserved.

BUT WHAT SAY I BOIL THAT SPAGHETTI FIRST?
IT IS A TAD FIRM

I'LL SEE YOU LATER, GARFIELD. I'M GOING TO THE SUPERMARKET
JIM DAVIS
8-17

LET'S SEE... I HAVE MY SHOPPING LIST, MY KEYS...
© 1982 PAWS, INC. All Rights Reserved.

DON'T FORGET YOUR SHOPPING BAG

SUPERMARKETS ARE LIKE A GIANT UNITED NATIONS OF FOOD
JIM DAVIS
8-18

YOU HAVE COFFEE FROM BRAZIL, CHEESE FROM FRANCE, BEEF FROM AUSTRALIA...

AND LASAGNA FROM HEAVEN
© 1982 PAWS, INC. All Rights Reserved.

© 1982 PAWS, INC. All Rights Reserved.

© 1982 PAWS, INC. All Rights Reserved.

© 1982 PAWS, INC. All Rights Reserved.

GARFIELD®

HOLY MOLEY!

HERE, BOY, SNIFF

CHOMP

RRRRRRR
ZIP
8-22

DOGS, YOU CAN'T LIVE WITH 'EM. YOU CAN'T LIVE WITHOUT 'EM
JIM DAVIS
©1982 PAWS, INC. All Rights Reserved.

I'M HUNGRY... NAH, I'M TOO TIRED TO BE HUNGRY... NAH, I'M TOO DEPRESSED TO BE TIRED
JIM DAVIS
8-23

YUP

IT'S MONDAY
© 1982 PAWS, INC. All Rights Reserved.

RATS...I CAN'T SHAKE THIS DEEP BLUE FUNK I'M IN
JIM DAVIS
8-24

NO DOUBT ABOUT IT...
© 1982 PAWS, INC. All Rights Reserved.

THIS WEEK IS GONNA BE ONE LONG MONDAY

OH BOY AM I DEPRESSED. I'M FAT, I'M LAZY, NOBODY LIKES ME...
JIM DAVIS
8-25

GOOD MORNING, OL' BUDDY. IT'S ANOTHER BEAUTIFUL DAY

QUIET. I'M ON A ROLL
© 1982 PAWS, INC. All Rights Reserved.

NOBODY LIKES ME
WHAT'S THE MATTER WITH YOU, GARFIELD?
JIM DAVIS
8-26

I SAID, NOBODY LIKES ME!
WHOCK!
BONK!

NOBODY LIKES ME, AND NOBODY LISTENS ANYMORE
© 1982 PAWS, INC. All Rights Reserved.

I'M STARTING TO LOSE MY DEPRESSION. I GOTTA DO SOMETHING
JIM DAVIS
8-27

© 1982 PAWS, INC. All Rights Reserved.

MUCH BETTER

I LOVE YOU, GARFIELD
LEAVE ME ALONE. I WANT TO BE DEPRESSED
JIM DAVIS
8-28

TICKLE! TICKLE! TICKLE!
HEE HEE
© 1982 PAWS, INC. All Rights Reserved.

FEEL BETTER, GARFIELD?
I'LL GET YOU FOR THIS, JON

©1982 PAWS, INC. All Rights Reserved.

LOOK OUT, WORLD! HERE COMES THE CAPED AVENGER!
JIM DAVIS
8-30

OH, SURE, SUPER-HERO CRIME FIGHTERS MAKE FOR AN OLD, OVERUSED STORY LINE...

BUT HAVE YOU EVER HEARD OF A FAT, WEAK ONE?
© 1982 PAWS, INC. All Rights Reserved.

THE CAPED AVENGER STEPS INTO THE SEAMY UNDERWORLD AND REASSERTS HIS NOBLE CODE
JIM DAVIS
8-31

"I WILL SEEK OUT EVIL WHEREVER IT MAY LURK AND DESTROY IT."

UNLESS, OF COURSE, THERE IS THE SLIGHTEST POSSIBILITY OF HARM TO MY PERSON
© 1982 PAWS, INC. All Rights Reserved.

JIM DAVIS
9-1

© 1982 PAWS, INC. All Rights Reserved.

DRIBBLE DRIBBLE DRIBBLE
THE CAPED AVENGER MUST PUMMEL THIS EVIL DOG
JIM DAVIS

9-2

DRIBBLE DRIBBLE DRIBBLE
THE CAPED AVENGER DISPLAYS A RARE SHOW OF COMPASSION
© 1982 PAWS, INC. All Rights Reserved.

THE CAPED AVENGER SPOTS SOME EVIL THAT MUST BE SEVERELY DEALT WITH
9-5
JIM DAVIS

WHAM!
BIFF!
BAM!

THE CAPED AVENGER WOULD BE A MORE EFFECTIVE CRIME FIGHTER IF HE DIDN'T HAVE TO USE ONE HAND TO HOLD HIS CAPE UP
© 1982 PAWS, INC. All Rights Reserved.

THIS CAPE IS THE SOURCE OF MY POWER, THE SOURCE OF MY IDENTITY
JIM DAVIS
9-4

THE SOURCE OF MY SECURITY
© 1982 PAWS, INC. All Rights Reserved.

GARFIELD®
JIM DAVIS
OH MY, WHAT A BEAUTIFUL BABY!
©1982 PAWS, INC. All Rights Reserved.
NORMALLY I DON'T LIKE BABIES...
BUT THIS ONE IS SPECIAL
I'M SUCH A SENTIMENTAL SLOB
9-5

THIS WEEK I'M GOING TO CHANGE MY WAYS. I'M GOING TO BEGIN BY NO LONGER HATING MONDAYS
JIM DAVIS
9-6

I'M CRAZY ABOUT MONDAYS. I JUST LOVE MONDAYS
© 1982 PAWS, INC. All Rights Reserved.

NOW I'M ONLY FOND OF MONDAYS

I RESOLVE TO STOP BEING FAT, LAZY AND CYNICAL. I SHALL NOW RISE AT AN EARLY HOUR
JIM DAVIS
9-7

Z
© 1982 PAWS, INC. All Rights Reserved.

AS LONG AS I'M IMPROVING MYSELF THIS WEEK, I MIGHT AS WELL TRY TO GET ALONG WITH ODIE
JIM DAVIS
9-8

COME HERE, ODIE. GIVE ME A BIG HUG
© 1982 PAWS, INC. All Rights Reserved.

YUK

I SHALL NOW USE SHEER WILLPOWER TO RESIST EATING THAT HAMBURGER
9-9
JIM DAVIS

UNNNGH

WAH!
I'M BEGINNING TO WORRY ABOUT GARFIELD
© 1982 PAWS, INC. All Rights Reserved.

THIS SELF-IMPROVEMENT BIT IS BEGINNING TO BUG ME. I FEEL LIKE A GOODY-TWO-SHOES
JIM DAVIS
9-10

MAYBE MY OLD PERSONALITY WASN'T ALL THAT BAD...

THE GLUTTONY, LAZINESS AND CYNICISM LENT A LITTLE TEXTURE
© 1982 PAWS, INC. All Rights Reserved.

I'M SICK OF THIS SELF-IMPROVEMENT KICK
9-11
JIM DAVIS

I'M FAT, I'M LAZY, AND I'M CYNICAL!

I ADMIRE THAT IN A CAT
© 1982 PAWS, INC. All Rights Reserved.

GARFIELD®

WHAP!

CHUKING

CATCH, GARFIELD

BONK!

EVER HAVE A DAY WHEN YOUR TIMING WAS ALL OFF?
JIM DAVIS 9-12
©1982 PAWS, INC. All Rights Reserved.

OH, NO!
JIM DAVIS
9-13

I AM DEFINITELY NOT GETTING OUT OF BED TODAY
© 1982 PAWS, INC. All Rights Reserved.

NOT ON MONDAY THE 13TH

JIM DAVIS
9-14

© 1982 PAWS, INC. All Rights Reserved.

YUK!
GARFIELD
JIM DAVIS
9-15

ALTHOUGH CATS ARE FINICKY EATERS...
GARFIELD
© 1982 PAWS, INC. All Rights Reserved.

"HUNGER STRIKE" ISN'T EXACTLY IN OUR VOCABULARY
GARFIELD

© 1982 PAWS, INC. All Rights Reserved.

© 1982 PAWS, INC. All Rights Reserved.

© 1982 PAWS, INC. All Rights Reserved.

GARFIELD®

ROOF
MEYOW

RAWF!
FFFT!
9-19
JIM DAVIS

BARK!
ROWR!

MROWR

BARK
©1982 PAWS, INC. All Rights Reserved.

YOU WIN

JIM DAVIS
9-20

© 1982 PAWS, INC. All Rights Reserved.

9-21
JIM DAVIS

SPLAT

A VERY SHORT BUT NEAT RAIN SHOWER
© 1982 PAWS, INC. All Rights Reserved.

JIM DAVIS
9-22

© 1982 PAWS, INC. All Rights Reserved.

PARDON ME. WHICH IS THE WAY TO CINCINNATI?
JIM DAVIS
9-23

THANKS
© 1982 PAWS, INC. All Rights Reserved.

I SEE BY THE OL' WRITING ON THE WALL IT'S TIME TO CHECK MYSELF INTO THE FUNNY FARM

JIM DAVIS
9-24

© 1982 PAWS, INC. All Rights Reserved.

LOOK AT ALL THOSE TINY ANTS GOING TO THE TINY BEACH TO DO SOME SWIMMING
JIM DAVIS
9-25

UH-OH. A TINY MINNOW IS CRUISING IN TO EAT THE SWIMMERS

UH-OH. THE MINNOW JUST GOT HARPOONED BY AN ANT WHO BEARS A STRIKING RESEMBLANCE TO ROBERT SHAW
© 1982 PAWS, INC. All Rights Reserved.

©1982 PAWS, INC. All Rights Reserved.

OH NO! IT'S NOT THERE!
JIM DAVIS
9-27

I'M NOT GETTING OUT OF BED WITHOUT IT!

NOT WITHOUT MY MORNING CUP OF COFFEE
© 1982 PAWS, INC. All Rights Reserved.

GOOD MORNING, JON
JIM DAVIS
9-28

WELL HELLOOOO THERE. COME TO PAPA

THAT'S ME, JON ARBUCKLE, SECOND FIDDLE TO A COFFEE BEAN
© 1982 PAWS, INC. All Rights Reserved.

GARFIELD, YOU'LL NEVER FIND HAPPINESS AT THE BOTTOM OF A COFFEE CUP
JIM DAVIS
9-29

I BEG TO DIFFER

LOOK, THERE'S SOME RIGHT THERE IN THE CORNER
BY GOLLY, YOU'RE RIGHT
© 1982 PAWS, INC. All Rights Reserved.

© 1982 PAWS, INC. All Rights Reserved.

©1982 PAWS, INC. All Rights Reserved.

© 1982 PAWS, INC. All Rights Reserved.

© 1982 PAWS, INC. All Rights Reserved.

© 1982 PAWS, INC. All Rights Reserved.

I WONDER WHAT THIS BAG OF SAWDUST HAS TO SAY
JIM DAVIS
10-7

FEED ME
FEED ME
FEED ME
FEED ME
FEED ME
© 1982 PAWS, INC. All Rights Reserved.

HE DOES HAVE A CERTAIN CHARM

IMAGINE, THE NERVE OF JON GIVING ME A DUMMY AS A COMPANION. WHAT KIND OF AN INTELLECTUAL DWARF DOES HE THINK I AM?
JIM DAVIS
10-8

PRACTICE OF THE ARISTOTELIAN MEAN WOULD HAVE A SIGNIFICANT POSITIVE EFFECT ON THE WORLD INSTITUTIONAL ENVIRONMENT
© 1982 PAWS, INC. All Rights Reserved.

OH, SHUT UP

YOUR LITTLE FRIEND HERE IS CERTAINLY CUTE, GARFIELD
JIM DAVIS
10-9

STOMP!
STOMP!
STOMP!

LITTLE FRIEND OR NOT, THERE'S SOMETHING TO BE SAID FOR THE DIPLOMATIC REMOVAL OF COMPETITION
© 1982 PAWS, INC. All Rights Reserved.

GARFIELD®

HERE'S AN INTERESTING ARTICLE ABOUT THE ANCIENT PRACTICE OF CANNIBALISM
LOVELY

CAN YOU IMAGINE WHAT LIFE WAS LIKE THEN?

TRAVELING SALESMEN WERE CALLED "MEALS ON WHEELS"

HAVING THE BOSS OVER FOR DINNER HAD AN ENTIRELY DIFFERENT MEANING

IT SAYS HERE CERTAIN TRIBAL SOCIETIES ALSO ATE CATS
©1982 PAWS, INC. All Rights Reserved.

I CAN HEAR A DINER COMPLAINING, "OH, WAITER, THERE'S A FLEA COLLAR IN MY SOUP"
THAT'S NOT FUNNY
JIM DAVIS
10-10

MAYBE I WOULDN'T HATE MONDAYS SO MUCH IF I DIDN'T HAVE THIS CALENDAR HERE TO REMIND ME
JIM DAVIS
10-11

© 1982 PAWS, INC. All Rights Reserved.

THAT HAMBURGER IS MINE, GARFIELD
IT'S MINE
JIM DAVIS
10-12

LET'S SEE IF YOU WANT IT AFTER I STOMP IT, LICK IT AND SHED ON IT

YOU WIN, GARFIELD. YOU CAN HAVE IT
I DON'T THINK I WANT IT NOW
© 1982 PAWS, INC. All Rights Reserved.

POP!
POP!
POP!
POP!
POP!
POP!
POP!

© 1982 PAWS, INC. All Rights Reserved.
LET ME GUESS. YOU'RE GOING TREE CLIMBING, RIGHT?

HOW DID YOU KNOW?
JIM DAVIS 10-13

© 1982 PAWS, INC. All Rights Reserved.

© 1982 PAWS, INC. All Rights Reserved.

© 1982 PAWS, INC. All Rights Reserved.

GARFIELD®

SMACK!

HEY!
©1982 PAWS, INC. All Rights Reserved.

TICKLE TICKLE TICKLE

STOP IT, GARFIELD! YOU PLAY TOO ROUGH!
JIM DAVIS 10-17

I'M SORRY I YELLED AT YOU, GARFIELD
CATS HAVE FEELINGS TOO, YOU KNOW

I'M NOT LEAVING BED, I'M NOT MOVING A MUSCLE. IF I DON'T BOTHER MONDAY, MAYBE MONDAY WON'T BOTHER ME
JIM DAVIS
10-18

HELLO, I'M NERMAL, THE WORLD'S CUTEST KITTEN, HERE TO VISIT FOR THE WEEK
© 1982 PAWS, INC. All Rights Reserved.

WELL, MAYBE I WILL DO JUST A TEENSY BIT OF SOBBING

THE MIRROR IS ONE OF CAT'S BEST FRIENDS, NERMAL. YOU CAN PRIMP IN IT, PLAY WITH IT AND ADMIRE YOURSELF IN IT
JIM DAVIS
10-19

© 1982 PAWS, INC. All Rights Reserved.

I DON'T SEE WHAT'S SO GREAT ABOUT IT

FOLLOW ME, NERMAL. THIS IS HOW YOU CLIMB A TREE
JIM DAVIS

NOW WHAT DO WE DO?
WHAT A SILLY QUESTION
10-20
© 1982 PAWS, INC. All Rights Reserved.

WE SIT HERE UNTIL THE FIRE DEPARTMENT COMES

LICK
JIM DAVIS
10-21

LICK
© 1982 PAWS, INC. All Rights Reserved.

WHAT HAPPENED TO YOU?

HOW CUTE. THANK YOU, NERMAL
JIM DAVIS
10-22

© 1982 PAWS, INC. All Rights Reserved.

UH... THANKS
YOU'D BETTER APPRECIATE IT, SUCKER. YOUR FLOWER GARDEN GAVE ITS LIFE FOR THIS BOUQUET

TELL ME, GARFIELD, ARE YOU THREATENED BY THE FACT THAT I AM MUCH YOUNGER AND CUTER THAN YOU ARE?
I'M BIGGER THAN THAT
JIM DAVIS
10-23

YOU CAN SAY THAT AGAIN!

SEE HOW THEY LIKE YOUR RAPIER WIT ON THE MOON
© 1982 PAWS, INC. All Rights Reserved.

© 1982 PAWS, INC. All Rights Reserved.

GET READY TO GO, GARFIELD. WE ARE GOING TO VISIT DAD AND MOM ON THE FARM
JIM DAVIS
10-25

SEND MY REGRETS. I REALLY MUST STAY HOME AND PLUCK MY NOSE HAIRS
© 1982 PAWS, INC. All Rights Reserved.

I GUESS I'M READY TO GO

JIM DAVIS
SPUT SPUT
WEEEZE
GURGLE
SPUT
© 1982 PAWS, INC. All Rights Reserved.
10-26

THE CAR HAS STOPPED AND IT'S GETTING DARK. WHAT SHOULD I DO, GARFIELD?
I CAN ONLY THINK OF ONE THING

MAKE IT GO!

WE'RE STRANDED, GARFIELD. WE'LL HAVE TO FIND SOMEWHERE TO SPEND THE NIGHT
JIM DAVIS
© 1982 PAWS, INC. All Rights Reserved.

WHAT ABOUT THAT PLACE?
CUTE
10-27

A LITTLE PAINT, A FEW CURTAINS, AND IT WOULD BE A REGULAR LOVE NEST

I GUESS WE'LL HAVE TO STAY IN THIS ABANDONED HOUSE TONIGHT, GARFIELD

GARFIELD
R.I.P.
6-19-78
10-30-82
© 1982 PAWS, INC. All Rights Reserved.
JIM DAVIS

I CAN'T PUT MY FINGER ON IT, BUT I HAVE AN UNEASY FEELING ABOUT THIS PLACE
GARFIELD
R.I.P.
6-19-78
10-30-82
10-28

THIS HOUSE IS SPOOKY, ISN'T IT, GARFIELD?
KIND OF REMINDS ME OF THE VET'S OFFICE

UH-OH, FOOTSTEPS! QUICK! INTO THE CLOSET!
CLOMP CLOMP
10-29
JIM DAVIS
© 1982 PAWS, INC. All Rights Reserved.

WHAT DO YOU SUPPOSE IT IS?
CLOMP CLOMP
LET'S HOPE IT'S THE WELCOME WAGON

IT'S COMING TO GET US, GARFIELD. IT KNOWS WE'RE IN THE CLOSET!
CLOMP CLOMP

ARRGH!

JIM DAVIS
10-30
DAD!
YOU DIDN'T SHOW, SO I CAME LOOKING FOR YOU
ONE LIFE DOWN, EIGHT TO GO
© 1982 PAWS, INC. All Rights Reserved.

© 1982 PAWS, INC. All Rights Reserved.

IT'S NICE TO BE BACK IN THE COUNTRY WITH SPACE TO ROAM

SPACE TO BREATHE, SPACE TO BE ME

SPACE TO BE BORED!
JIM DAVIS 11-1
© 1982 PAWS, INC. All Rights Reserved.

I THINK I'LL HAVE AN EGG FOR BREAKFAST
JIM DAVIS
11-2

CRACK!
© 1982 PAWS, INC. All Rights Reserved.

MOMMY!
MAYBE CHICKEN FOR LUNCH

MOMMY!
JIM DAVIS
11-3

LOOK, KID, I'M NOT YOUR MOMMY. I'M A BOY. BOYS CAN'T BE MOMMIES

DADDY!
© 1982 PAWS, INC. All Rights Reserved.

WHAT'S THAT, DADDY?
IT'S LASAGNA. AND DON'T CALL ME DADDY
JIM DAVIS
11-4

HERE, HAVE A PIECE
YUK!

NO SON OF MINE WOULD REFUSE LASAGNA!
© 1982 PAWS, INC. All Rights Reserved.

STOP HANGING AROUND ME, KID. JUST REMEMBER, YOU'RE A TENDER YOUNG CHICKEN AND I'M A VERY HUNGRY CAT
JIM DAVIS
11-5

I GUESS I GAVE THAT LITTLE GIBLET THE WHAT FOR

EYOW!
© 1982 PAWS, INC. All Rights Reserved.

FOR THE LAST TIME, KID, I'M NOT YOUR DADDY. YOU'RE A CHICKEN AND I'M A CAT
JIM DAVIS
11-6

NOW GO BACK TO YOUR MOTHER
GOODBYE, DADDY

© 1982 PAWS, INC. All Rights Reserved.

© 1982 PAWS, INC. All Rights Reserved.

GARFIELD'S LAW: CATS MOVE AT A SPEED PROPORTIONATE TO THE AMOUNT OF FOOD AT THEIR DESTINATION. THEY MAY EVEN EXCEED THE SPEED OF SOUND
GARFIELD
11-8
JIM DAVIS
© 1982 PAWS, INC. All Rights Reserved.
MEOW

GARFIELD'S LAW: CATS ARE INDEPENDENT. CATS ARE LONERS...
11-9
JIM DAVIS
© 1982 PAWS, INC. All Rights Reserved.
THEY ARE UNDERFOOT ONLY WHEN YOU'RE CARRYING GROCERIES
SORRY ABOUT THAT

GARFIELD'S LAW: CATS INSTINCTIVELY KNOW THE PRECISE MOMENT THEIR OWNERS WILL AWAKE...
JIM DAVIS
© 1982 PAWS, INC. All Rights Reserved.
11-10
THEN THEY AWAKEN THEM TEN MINUTES SOONER

GARFIELD'S LAW: CATS ARE NATURALLY ATTRACTED TO ONLY ONE TYPE OF HUMAN BEING...
11-11

JIM DAVIS
© 1982 PAWS, INC. All Rights Reserved.

THE TYPE WHO IS ALLERGIC TO CATS
WAHCHOO!

GARFIELD'S LAW: CATS CAN'T HEAR COMMANDS...
GARFIELD! GET OFF THE BED!
JIM DAVIS 11-12

CATS CAN'T UNDERSTAND CAJOLING...
SEE? EVEN TOMMY THE CLOWN LIKES THIS NEW CAT FOOD
GARFIEL
© 1982 PAWS, INC. All Rights Reserved.

BUT THEY DO SENSE WHEN YOU WANT TO TAKE THEM TO THE VET
LET'S GO FOR A RIDE, GARFIELD

GARFIELD'S LAW: CATS SHED IN DIRECT PROPORTION TO THEIR CONTRAST WITH A PERSON'S SUIT
JIM DAVIS
11-13

© 1982 PAWS, INC. All Rights Reserved.

© 1982 PAWS, INC. All Rights Reserved.

© 1982 PAWS, INC. All Rights Reserved.

© 1982 PAWS, INC. All Rights Reserved.

© 1982 PAWS, INC. All Rights Reserved.

I HATE CUTE
JIM DAVIS
11-18

© 1982 PAWS, INC. All Rights Reserved.

I ALSO HATE PEOPLE WHO TRY TO INGRATIATE THEMSELVES

KONK!
CHUKING
JIM DAVIS
11-19

I HATE TOASTERS

KRONK
CHUKING
© 1982 PAWS, INC. All Rights Reserved.

I HATE HATING THINGS
11-20
JIM DAVIS

CHECK THAT

I LOVE HATING DOGS
PUNT!
© 1982 PAWS, INC. All Rights Reserved.

GARFIELD®

I WISH DOCTORS WOULDN'T LEAVE THEIR INSTRUMENTS SITTING OUT

JUST AS I THOUGHT, IT'S ICY COLD

I WONDER WHAT SHE INTENDS TO SNIP OFF WITH THIS?
© 1982 PAWS, INC. All Rights Reserved.

I DON'T EVEN WANT TO KNOW WHERE THIS GOES

HELLO, GARFIELD
ARRRGH!
JIM DAVIS

HE'S FAINTED DEAD AWAY
HE'S DADDY'S LITTLE TROOPER
11-21

11-22
JIM DAVIS

OH, GEE, I CAN'T GET INTO MY BED WITH THESE MUDDY FEET
© 1982 PAWS, INC. All Rights Reserved.

Z

I LOVE TO SLEEP. I SLEEP TO RESTORE MY ENERGY
JIM DAVIS
11-23

I SLEEP TO REFRESH MY WITS

I SLEEP TO ESCAPE
© 1982 PAWS, INC. All Rights Reserved.

JIM DAVIS
11-24

Z
© 1982 PAWS, INC. All Rights Reserved.

GARFIELD! WHAT HAPPENED?
I HAD A NAP ATTACK AT FULL THROTTLE

IF I WERE TO COME BACK TO THIS EARTH, I'D LIKE TO COME BACK AS A PILLOW
JIM DAVIS

I COULD LIE IN BED ALL DAY
© 1982 PAWS, INC. All Rights Reserved.
11-25

AND PEOPLE WOULD PUT THEIR HEADS IN MY LAP AND GO TO SLEEP

UH-OH! HERE COMES THAT MEAN DOG!
JIM DAVIS
11-26

NOBODY WOULD EVER HARM A SLEEPING CAT

WRONGO
© 1982 PAWS, INC. All Rights Reserved.

JIM DAVIS
11-27

Z
Z
© 1982 PAWS, INC. All Rights Reserved.

MY FEET FELL ASLEEP
Z
Z

GARFIELD®

Z
DUM DEE DUM DEE DUM

YAH TAH TAH TAH, YAH TAH TAH TAH
TAP
TAP
TAP
TAP
TAP
JIM DAVIS

GARFIELD, I WAS SOUND ASLEEP
YOU'RE BREAKING MY HEART. NOW FEED ME
11-28

ANYTHING ELSE, SIRE?
YES, WASH MY BLANKET, CHANGE MY KITTY LITTER AND RETREAD MY SCRATCHING POST

I WONDER IF IT'S WORTH IT
I'LL IGNORE THAT REMARK
© 1982 PAWS, INC. All Rights Reserved.

I SWEAR. SOMETIMES I DON'T KNOW WHY I KEEP HIM

SNAP!
SQUEAK!
WHAT'S THAT?
JIM DAVIS
11-29

OH, NO! SINCE I'M NOT A MOUSER, JON SET A MOUSETRAP. NOW IT'S KILLED A MOUSE!
© 1982 PAWS, INC. All Rights Reserved.

IF YOU DID YOUR JOB, I WOULDN'T BE IN THIS FIX

I'M SORRY YOU GOT CAUGHT IN THAT MOUSETRAP, MOUSE
OH, THAT'S OKAY. I HAVE A WIFE AND EIGHT KIDS
JIM DAVIS
11-30

WHAT DOES THAT HAVE TO DO WITH ANYTHING?

THIS IS THE FIRST PEACE AND QUIET I'VE HAD IN YEARS
© 1982 PAWS, INC. All Rights Reserved.

HAVE A PIECE OF CHEESE, MOUSE. MAYBE THAT WILL MAKE YOU FEEL BETTER
JIM DAVIS
12-1

© 1982 PAWS, INC. All Rights Reserved.

HOW AM I SUPPOSED TO SWALLOW?
GOOD POINT

YOU'RE FREE TO GO, MOUSE
THANKS
JIM DAVIS

JUST WHERE HAVE YOU BEEN? I SUPPOSE YOU AND YOUR FAT FRIEND HAVE BEEN HAVING FUN WHILE I'VE BEEN WORKING AND SLAVING TAKING CARE OF OUR CHILDREN. YOU'D BETTER GET YOURSELF HOME RIGHT NOW
© 1982 PAWS, INC. All Rights Reserved.

SNAP!
12-2

NOW GET OUT OF HERE

© 1982 PAWS, INC. All Rights Reserved.

SNAP!
SQUEAK!
JIM DAVIS
12-3

JON WILL BE CHECKING THIS TRAP SOON
© 1982 PAWS, INC. All Rights Reserved.

MY BUNNY SLIPPERS?
THEY LIKE TO ROAM AT NIGHT
12-4
JIM DAVIS

GARFIELD®

I LOVE FLOWERS!

I LOVE TO TIPTOE THROUGH TULIPS

DIVE THROUGH DAISIES

JIM DAVIS 12-5
ROMP THROUGH ROSES

YOUR CAT BROKE'M, YOU BOUGHT'EM, BUDDY
Floral Shoppe
PUT SOME PANSIES ON THE TAB, TOO
© 1982 PAWS, INC. All Rights Reserved.

© 1982 PAWS, INC. All Rights Reserved.

© 1982 PAWS, INC. All Rights Reserved.

© 1982 PAWS, INC. All Rights Reserved.

JIM DAVIS
12-9

MY NEWSPAPER! YOU CHEWED UP MY NEWSPAPER!

IT'S THINGS LIKE THIS THAT MAKE ME WONDER IF YOU SHOULD BRING IN THE PAPER AT ALL
PRECISELY
POO
© 1982 PAWS, INC. All Rights Reserved.

ON CHILLY MORNINGS, THIS IS MY FAVORITE PLACE IN THE WHOLE HOUSE
12-10
JIM DAVIS

OVER THE HEAT VENT
© 1982 PAWS, INC. All Rights Reserved.

GARFIELD, DID YOU EAT MY FERN?
© 1982 PAWS, INC. All Rights Reserved.

WHY IS IT I GET BLAMED FOR EVERYTHING AROUND HERE? IF SOMETHING GOES WRONG, YOU JUST LAY IT ON OL'GARFIELD!
12-11
JIM DAVIS

I HAVE NO IDEA WHAT YOU'RE TALKING ABOUT

© 1982 PAWS, INC. All Rights Reserved.

BOOM
BOOM
BOOM
JIM DAVIS
12-13

BOOM
BOOM
BOOM

IT'S TIME YOU WENT ON ANOTHER DIET, GARFIELD
© 1982 PAWS, INC. All Rights Reserved.

ON THIS DIET, GARFIELD, YOU MAY DRINK ALL THE COFFEE YOU PLEASE
JIM DAVIS
12-14

GULP
GULP
GULP

THIS IS SOME KIND OF WEIRD DIET
SLOSH
SLOSH
SLOSH
SLOSH
© 1982 PAWS, INC. All Rights Reserved.

I THINK I'LL STEP OFF MY DIET JUST LONG ENOUGH TO EAT A COUPLE DOZEN COOKIES
JIM DAVIS
12-15

LETTUCE ?!

THAT CAT HAS NO SENSE OF HUMOR
© 1982 PAWS, INC. All Rights Reserved.

JIM DAVIS
© 1982 PAWS, INC. All Rights Reserved.
12-16

YOU KNOW YOU'RE ON A DIET WHEN EVEN THE DOG FOOD COMMERCIALS LOOK GOOD

YOU MAY GO OFF YOUR DIET AS SOON AS YOU LOSE SOME WEIGHT, GARFIELD
WHY DIDN'T YOU SAY SO SOONER?
JIM DAVIS
12-17

BUZZ
©1982 PAWS, INC. All Rights Reserved.

LET'S EAT

HECK WITH IT. I'M GOING OFF MY DIET
12-18
JIM DAVIS

© 1982 PAWS, INC. All Rights Reserved.

SHOW ME A DIETER, AND I'LL SHOW YOU A PERSON WHO BELITTLES HIMSELF

GARFIELD®

GOOD MORNING, GARFIELD. I'M SO HAPPY YOU CAN SHARE THIS GLORIOUS MORNING WITH ME

MICHELANGELO WOULD GIVE UP PAINTING IN A MINUTE. IF HE SAW THE CANVAS MOTHER NATURE HAS RENDERED JUST FOR US TODAY

CHIRP CHIRP
JUST LISTEN TO THE SYMPHONY OF SOUND FROM NATURE'S FLUTE SECTION

AND THE PERFECT SIGHTS AND SOUNDS ARE PERFUMED WITH THESE LOVELY FLOWERS. WHAT DO YOU THINK, GARFIELD?

JIM DAVIS
12-19

YOU REALLY DON'T CARE, DO YOU?
BINGO
© 1982 PAWS, INC. All Rights Reserved.

© 1982 PAWS, INC. All Rights Reserved.

© 1982 PAWS, INC. All Rights Reserved.

© 1982 PAWS, INC. All Rights Reserved.

I HOPE THIS GIFT IS MINE
RATTLE RATTLE
RATTLE
JIM DAVIS

CRACK!
TINKLE TINKLE
TINKLE
12-23

I HOPE IT'S ODIE'S
© 1982 PAWS, INC. All Rights Reserved.

IT'S ONLY NOON, GARFIELD. ARE YOU GOING TO BED ALREADY?
THE SOONER YOU GO TO BED, THE SOONER IT'S CHRISTMAS MORNING
JIM DAVIS
12-24

© 1982 PAWS, INC. All Rights Reserved.

GOOD NIGHT, LITTLE FELLA

COMICS READERS ARE VERY SPECIAL PEOPLE. YOU MEAN MORE TO ME THAN THERE IS SPACE HERE TO EXPRESS

I LOVE YOU ALL
© 1982 PAWS, INC. All Rights Reserved.

HAVE A HAPPY HOLIDAY. I'LL BE FUNNY AGAIN TOMORROW, TRUST ME
JIM DAVIS 12-25

GARFIELD®

GOOD EVENING, LADIES AND GERMS

SPLAT
© 1982 PAWS, INC. All Rights Reserved.

MY CAR IS SO OLD, IT IS INSURED AGAINST FIRE, THEFT AND INDIAN RAIDS
BLUT

MY GIRLFRIEND IS SO CROSS-EYED, SHE CAN SIT ON THE FRONT PORCH AND COUNT THE CHICKENS IN THE BACKYARD
CRASH

TAKE MY DOG... PLEEEZE
PLOP
12-26

IT MUST HAVE BEEN ONE OF YOUR BETTER NIGHTS
I WAS IN RARE FORM
JIM DAVIS

WELL, I WONDER WHAT'S GOING TO HAPPEN TO ME TODAY
JIM DAVIS
12-27

BLAT!
© 1982 PAWS, INC. All Rights Reserved.

MONDAY MOVES IN A MYSTERIOUS WAY

GO FETCH THE PAPER, GARFIELD
12-28
JIM DAVIS

LOOK CLOSELY, JON. THESE ARE CAT'S PAWS, NOT SLAVE'S PAWS
© 1982 PAWS, INC. All Rights Reserved.

I'LL IGNORE YOUR SMALL INDISCRETION THIS TIME, AND SPARE YOUR LIFE
THANK YOU, ... SIR

NIBBLE
NIBBLE
NIBBLE
12-29
JIM DAVIS

IT'S NOT GOOD TO CHEW YOUR NAILS, GARFIELD
OH, THAT'S OKAY

I'M CHEWING ON ODIE'S
© 1982 PAWS, INC. All Rights Reserved.

Z
JIM DAVIS
12-30

I'M BORED. I NEED TO ADD SOME SPARKLE TO MY LIFE

Z
© 1982 PAWS, INC. All Rights Reserved.

THERE'S A SPIDER! I HATE SPIDERS!
HA HA. I'LL JUST FLICK HIM AWAY
JIM DAVIS
12-31

WHANG!

JON? ARE YOU OKAY?... JON?
© 1982 PAWS, INC. All Rights Reserved.

JIM DAVIS
1-1-83

ZOOM!

THE EARLY CAT GETS THE JELLY-FILLED DONUT
© 1963 PAWS, INC. All Rights Reserved.

© 1983 PAWS, INC. All Rights Reserved.

BRINNNG!
JIM DAVIS
1-3-83

WHAM!
©1983 PAWS, INC. All Rights Reserved.

BRINNNG!

JIM DAVIS
1-4-83

I DIDN'T KNOW YOU LIKE TO DANCE, GARFIELD
WHAT ARE YOU TALKING ABOUT?

I WAS SCRATCHING MY BACK WITH YOUR TOOTHBRUSH
©1983 PAWS, INC. All Rights Reserved.

GOOD MORNING, ODIE
JIM DAVIS
1-5-83

HEY, GET AWAY FROM JON'S STAMP COLLECTION!

TOO LATE
©1983 PAWS, INC. All Rights Reserved.

WHAT SHOULD I DO TONIGHT?
1-6-83
JIM DAVIS

SPLUT
©1983 PAWS, INC. All Rights Reserved.

GOOD IDEA. I THINK I'LL GO SING ON THE FENCE

OH, NO! FIRE ARROWS!
THOCK
1-7-83

I'M A GONER!
THOCK
©1983 PAWS, INC. All Rights Reserved.

A CAT ALWAYS GOES DOWN WITH HIS FENCE!
JIM DAVIS

I CAN'T BELIEVE THAT TACKY PACK OF MUSIC HATERS BURNED MY FENCE DOWN
1-8-83
JIM DAVIS

THE ONLY THING TO DO IS TO GET RIGHT BACK UP THERE AND START SINGING AGAIN
©1983 PAWS, INC. All Rights Reserved.

BUT... SOMEHOW IT JUST ISN'T THE SAME

GARFIELD®
HEY, ODIE, WOULD YOU LIKE TO PLAY BALL?
SQUEAK
© 1983 PAWS, INC. All Rights Reserved.
TIE
TIE
HEY, GARFIELD. WHERE'S ODIE?
HE'S TIED UP AT THE MOMENT
DRIBBLE
DRIBBLE
DRIBBLE
JIM DAVIS
1-9

SLAM
1-10
JIM DAVIS

HEY, GARFIELD. I'M HOME

YOU'RE CERTAINLY EXCITED TO SEE ME
BELIEVE ME, INSIDE I'M HOPPING UP AND DOWN AND SHOUTING WITH GLEE
© 1983 PAWS, INC. All Rights Reserved.

SO I SAY TO THIS CLERK, "LOOK, IF THE WHOLE BUNCH OF BANANAS IS 54 CENTS, WHY CAN'T I HAVE ONE FOR 6 CENTS?"
1-11
JIM DAVIS

© 1983 PAWS, INC. All Rights Reserved.

DON'T YOU WANT TO HEAR HOW THE STORY CAME OUT?
TELL IT TO YOUR PLANTS

1-12
JIM DAVIS

GARFIELD, YOU SEEM TO BE PREOCCUPIED THIS WEEK
HUH?
© 1983 PAWS, INC. All Rights Reserved.

GARFIELD HASN'T BEEN LISTENING TO ME LATELY. WATCH THIS
1-13
JIM DAVIS

HEY, GARFIELD, WHAT SAY WE GO TO THE VET AND GET YOU DECLAWED?

THAT WOULD BE FINE
CASE CLOSED
©1983 PAWS, INC. All Rights Reserved.

I HATE IT WHEN GARFIELD IGNORES ME
1-14
JIM DAVIS

DARN IT! PAY SOME ATTENTION TO ME!

Z
I THINK I'M GOING TO CRY
©1983 PAWS, INC. All Rights Reserved.

JON, I KNOW I'VE BEEN IGNORING YOU LATELY, BUT I WANT TO SAY IT'S NOT BECAUSE I DON'T CARE FOR YOU
1-15

IT'S LIKE MY EARS HEAR YOU, BUT MY BRAIN KEEPS STRAYING OFF COURSE. I'VE JUST BEEN PREOCCUPIED
JIM DAVIS
©1983 PAWS, INC. All Rights Reserved.

ENOUGH SAID. LET'S GET ON WITH IT
HUH?

GARFIELD®

I WONDER WHAT IT WOULD BE LIKE TO BE A WILD ANIMAL
DO NOT FEED THE ANIMALS
ZOO
© 1983 PAWS, INC. All Rights Reserved.

FIRST, I'D ALTER THIS STUPID SIGN
DO NOT
FEED THE ANIMALS

THEN I'D PACE AROUND LOOKING KINDA FIERCE
FEED THE ANIMALS
JIM DAVIS
1-16

THEN I'D SCARE THE HECK OUT OF THE CROWD

EEEEK!
SWIPE

THAT WAS A PRETTY CONVINCING PERFORMANCE, IF I DO SAY SO MYSELF

JIM DAVIS
1-17

©1983 PAWS, INC. All Rights Reserved.

I LOVE IT WHEN THEY ENTERTAIN ME

IT APPEARS JON HAS PREPARED HIMSELF A VERY NICE MEAL, BUT SOMETHING IS MISSING. WHAT COULD IT BE?
JIM DAVIS
1-18

WHY, OF COURSE...
©1983 PAWS, INC. All Rights Reserved.

THE CAT HAIR!

JIM DAVIS
1-19

©1983 PAWS, INC. All Rights Reserved.

OKAY, OKAY, I'LL TURN THE HEAT UP

THIS IS MY HUMBLE ABODE, MY DEAR
JIM DAVIS 1-20

© 1983 PAWS, INC. All Rights Reserved.

WHO WERE THEY?
OH, JUST A COUPLE OF ANIMALS I'M GIVING AWAY SOON

GARFIELD, SOMETIMES I THINK YOU DON'T LIKE IT WHEN I HAVE DATES
ABSOLUTELY
JIM DAVIS
1-21

DATING LEADS TO MARRIAGE. MARRIAGE LEADS TO CHILDREN

AND DO YOU KNOW WHAT CHILDREN DO TO CATS?
© 1983 PAWS, INC. All Rights Reserved.

HEY, JON, WHAT'S HAPPENING?
JIM DAVIS

EAT YOUR BREAKFAST, GARFIELD
1-22

WHERE'S YOUR SENSE OF HUMOR?
© 1983 PAWS, INC. All Rights Reserved.

GARFIELD®
ISN'T THAT HALLEY'S COMET?!
ZIP!
GARFIELD, DID YOU TAKE MY STEAK?
WHO? LITTLE OL'ME?
JIM DAVIS
1-23
LOOK, I DON'T HAVE YOUR CRUMMY OLD STEAK
HEY! I DON'T HAVE YOUR CRUMMY OLD STEAK!
I'M GOING TO GET YOU FOR THIS, ODIE
BURP
©1983 PAWS, INC. All Rights Reserved.

PLAYING WITH A BALL OF YARN IS A GREAT WAY TO GET ATTENTION
1-24
JIM DAVIS

THOCK!
© 1983 PAWS, INC. All Rights Reserved.

GARFIELD!
TAH DAH

HEY, GARFIELD, THERE'S A LASAGNA UNDER THE BED!
JIM DAVIS

© 1983 PAWS, INC. All Rights Reserved.

THANKS FOR DUSTING UNDER THE BED FOR ME, GARFIELD
I HATE YOU
1-25

JIM DAVIS

© 1983 PAWS, INC. All Rights Reserved.
WHIRRR!

NIGHTIE-NIGHT, JON
I HATE YOU
1-26

SURPRISE, GARFIELD! I BOUGHT YOU ANOTHER RUBBER MOUSE
YIPPEE SKIP
JIM DAVIS

BY THE WAY, WHAT HAPPENED TO YOUR LAST ONE?
IT WAS TRAGIC

HE WAS CAUGHT AND EATEN BY A RUBBER CAT
©1983 PAWS, INC. All Rights Reserved.
1-27

SURPRISE, GARFIELD! I THREW YOUR OLD BED IN THE TRASH AND GOT YOU THIS NEW ONE. WHAT DO YOU THINK?
JIM DAVIS

1-28

©1983 PAWS, INC. All Rights Reserved.
Z

DOGS HAVE THE WORLD'S STUPIDEST TOYS. JUST LOOK AT THIS RUBBER BONE
JIM DAVIS

SIMPLE MINDS, SIMPLE PLEASURES

IT CERTAINLY DOESN'T HOLD THE SCINTILLATING INTELLECTUAL CHALLENGE OF MY FUZZY SCRATCHING POST WITH THE SPRINGY RUBBER MOUSIE
1-29
©1983 PAWS, INC. All Rights Reserved.

GARFIELD®

© 1983 PAWS, INC. All Rights Reserved.

JIM DAVIS 1-30

COFFEE

ROWR!
ARRRGH!
COFFEE

THAT WASN'T FUNNY, GARFIELD!
FUNNY IS IN THE EYE OF THE BEHOLDER
COFFEE

PLOP!

EEEEEEK!
JIM DAVIS
1-31

I'M ALMOST AFRAID TO ASK WHAT HAPPENED HERE
©1983 PAWS, INC. All Rights Reserved.

QUICK! QUICK! PUT POOKY'S ARM BACK ON!
JIM DAVIS

RELAX, GARFIELD. I'LL FIX POOKY RIGHT UP. IT'S NO BIG DEAL
2-1
©1983 PAWS, INC. All Rights Reserved.

NO BIG DEAL?! LOOK, BUSTER, I'VE NEVER LOST A LOVED ONE BEFORE

2-2
JIM DAVIS

I SEWED POOKY'S ARM BACK ON AS GOOD AS NEW, GARFIELD

YES, BUT WILL HE EVER PLAY THE PIANO AGAIN?
ME THINKS THE CAT DOTH EXPECT TOO MUCH
©1983 PAWS, INC. All Rights Reserved.

YOU DID A PRETTY GOOD JOB OF SEWING POOKY'S ARM ON
2-3
JIM DAVIS

I USED SMALL STITCHES SO AS NOT TO LEAVE A SCAR

I THINK HE'S PICKING ON ME
©1983 PAWS, INC. All Rights Reserved.

POOKY, WHEN YOU LOST YOUR ARM, I GOT TO THINKING ABOUT OUR MORTALITY, AND THAT'S DEPRESSING
2-4
JIM DAVIS

SO PROMISE ME YOU'LL NEVER LOSE YOUR ARM AGAIN, OKAY?

©1983 PAWS, INC. All Rights Reserved.

I WONDER WHAT MY FORTUNE COOKIE FORTUNE IS
JIM DAVIS
2-5

TODAY YOU WILL BE WHISKED AWAY TO A LARGE WHITE BUILDING WHERE ALL YOU HAVE TO DO IS LIE IN BED ALL DAY AS LOTS OF PEOPLE PAY ATTENTION TO YOU AND BRING YOU FOOD

©1983 PAWS, INC. All Rights Reserved.
THAT SOUNDS TOO GOOD TO BE TRUE

GARFIELD®

I CAN STARE ANYTHING DOWN
© 1983 PAWS, INC. All Rights Reserved.

UH, GARFIELD, FISH CAN'T BLINK
JIM DAVIS
2-6

NOW HE TELLS ME... NOW THAT MY EYEBALLS ARE ALL DRIED OUT

I WONDER WHAT AWFUL THING IS GOING TO HAPPEN TO ME TODAY? MAYBE THE SKY WILL FALL. MAYBE ODIE WILL BRING HIS LONG LOST TWIN BROTHER HOME...
JIM DAVIS
2-7
OR WORSE YET, MAYBE NERMAL WILL COME FOR A VISIT
©1983 PAWS, INC. All Rights Reserved.

OH SURE, YOU'RE GETTING ALL THE ATTENTION RIGHT NOW, NERMAL. BUT WHEN YOU GROW UP YOU'LL BE AS UNLOVED AS I AM
JIM DAVIS
2-8
I'M NEVER GROWING UP
WHO ARE YOU? PETER PAN OR SOMETHING?
I'M A MIDGET
SOME CATS GET ALL THE LUCK
©1983 PAWS, INC. All Rights Reserved.

IF YOU WANT TO BE CUTE LIKE ME, YOU HAVE TO PLAY WITH A BALL OF YARN
THAT SOUNDS SIMPLE ENOUGH
JIM DAVIS
2-9
YOURS IS OVER THERE
I HATE HIM
©1983 PAWS, INC. All Rights Reserved.

NERMAL, YOU'RE SO SWEET, WHY DON'T I JUST STUFF YOU INTO THIS SUGAR BOWL
JIM DAVIS
2-10

GO AHEAD AND TRY IT, FAT BOY
©1983 PAWS, INC. All Rights Reserved.

SAY, GARFIELD, WHERE'S NERMAL?
AT A HUMILITY LESSON

YOU DISGUST ME, NERMAL
JIM DAVIS
2-11

YOU'RE A WIDE-EYED, MINDLESS LITTLE PIECE OF FLUFF. YOU'RE SO CUTE EVERYONE LOVES YOU

EAT YOUR HEART OUT, BOZO
I AM, I AM
©1983 PAWS, INC. All Rights Reserved.

YOU'VE OVERSTAYED YOUR WELCOME
UNK
GARFIELD
2-12

GARFIELD
©1983 PAWS, INC. All Rights Reserved.

WHERE'S NERMAL?
YOU KNOW... IT WAS STRANGE, HE MUTTERED "UNK" AND THEN LEFT WITHOUT A WORD
JIM DAVIS
GARFIELD

GARFIELD®

GARFIELD, WHY DON'T YOU LIKE TO TAKE BATHS?
BATHING ROBS CATS OF PRECIOUS NATURAL OILS THAT PROTECT US FROM SKIN DISEASE

WHAT DO YOU KNOW? HOP IN THERE RIGHT NOW
LET ME GET MY TUBBY TOYS

TODAY, TODAY

THERE NOW, DON'T YOU FEEL MUCH BETTER?
MUCH
JIM DAVIS 2-13
© 1983 PAWS, INC. All Rights Reserved.

ARE YOU SURE YOU WANT TO WATCH THIS, GARFIELD?
JIM DAVIS

IT'S A DEPRESSING MOVIE ABOUT A MAN-EATING LION THAT TERRORIZES A NATIVE VILLAGE
2-14
©1983 PAWS, INC. All Rights Reserved.

YOU ROOT FOR YOUR SIDE, I'LL ROOT FOR MINE
LION

I HATE MOVIES ABOUT MAN-EATING LIONS
JIM DAVIS

HOW CAN AN ANIMAL POSSIBLY PREY ON AN INNOCENT VICTIM?
2-15
©1983 PAWS, INC. All Rights Reserved.

EXPLAIN THAT TO THE CHICKEN YOU HAD FOR DINNER

OH, NO! THE LION RAN DOWN ANOTHER VILLAGER!
THE ORIGINAL FAST-FOOD FRANCHISE
JIM DAVIS

NOW WHAT DISGUSTING THING IS THE LION DOING?
2-16
©1983 PAWS, INC. All Rights Reserved.

HE'S SPITTING THE SPEAR OUT

TELL ME WHEN THE LION IS FINISHED EATING THE VILLAGER, OKAY, GARFIELD?
YOU CAN LOOK NOW
JIM DAVIS
EEEEEK!
2-17
HE WASN'T DONE YET!
OH, I THOUGHT YOU MEANT THE MAIN PARTS
©1983 PAWS, INC. All Rights Reserved.

GOOD! THEY SHOT THE LION!
JIM DAVIS
WHAT DO YOU THINK OF THOSE APPLES, GARFIELD?
BIG DEAL
2-18
AT THE GUN IT WAS VILLAGERS: 1, LION: 42
©1983 PAWS, INC. All Rights Reserved.

WELL, WHAT DID YOU THINK OF THE MAN-EATING LION MOVIE?
JIM DAVIS
2-19
YOU KNOW I HATE THAT, GARFIELD
©1983 PAWS, INC. All Rights Reserved.

GARFIELD®

ICE, ONE. ODIE, NOTHING
BAP!
© 1983 PAWS, INC. All Rights Reserved.

WATCH THIS
JIM DAVIS

AIR MAIL!
2-20

HAVE A NICE TRIP, JON!

OH NO!

MY TOMATO PASTE!

© 1983 PAWS, INC. All Rights Reserved.

I'D BETTER SAVE SOME OF THIS BLUEBERRY PIE FOR JON. TO EAT IT ALL WOULD BE INCONSIDERATE AND SELFISH
JIM DAVIS
2-24

I AM WHAT I AM
©1983 PAWS, INC. All Rights Reserved.

THIS IS CALLED A BIRD FEEDER, GARFIELD
JIM DAVIS
2-25

AND THIS IS CALLED PUTTING BIRDSEED INTO THE BIRD FEEDER

HE CAN CALL IT WHAT HE LIKES. I CALL IT BAITING THE TRAP
©1983 PAWS, INC. All Rights Reserved.

WOW! LOOK AT ALL THIS GOOD FOOD AND NEAT CLOTHING!
2-26

THIS IS GREAT STUFF
©1983 PAWS, INC. All Rights Reserved.

STAY OUT OF THE TRASH, GARFIELD
HOW DID YOU KNOW?
JIM DAVIS

© 1983 PAWS, INC. All Rights Reserved.

I HATE MONDAYS
JIM DAVIS
2-28

MAYBE IF I TORE MONDAYS OFF THE CALENDAR THERE'D BE NO MORE MONDAYS
RIP!
©1983 PAWS, INC. All Rights Reserved.

THERE MUST BE AN EASIER WAY TO EAT
3-1
JIM DAVIS

GO AHEAD AND START WITHOUT ME, BREAKFAST
GARFIELD

BURP... I SHOULD HAVE THOUGHT OF THAT LONG AGO
©1983 PAWS, INC. All Rights Reserved.

WHAT A UNIQUE PERSPECTIVE. NOW THE CEILING IS THE FLOOR, AND THE FLOOR IS THE CEILING
HI, GARFIELD
3-2
JIM DAVIS

ZIP
©1983 PAWS, INC. All Rights Reserved.

WHATEVER GOES DOWN, MUST COME UP

© 1983 PAWS, INC. All Rights Reserved.

© 1983 PAWS, INC. All Rights Reserved.

GARFIELD

I THINK I'LL MOVE IN SLOW-MOTION TODAY

WHA!?

JIM DAVIS

OH, NO, YOU DON'T

IT'S HARD TO TAKE WHAT YOU WANT IN LIFE WHEN THEY SEE YOU COMING
© 1983 PAWS, INC. All Rights Reserved.
3-6

UH-OH, THERE'S A PACKAGE FOR ME
JIM DAVIS
3-7

I DON'T THINK I'M GOING TO LIKE IT

BEWARE OF GIFTS BEARING AIR HOLES
© 1983 PAWS, INC. All Rights Reserved.

GEE, I HOPE THIS PACKAGE DOESN'T HAVE A BOMB OR A MONSTER IN IT
JIM DAVIS
3-8

GASP! IT'S EVEN WORSE THAN MY MOST HIDEOUS FEARS!

IT'S ANOTHER SWEATER FOR ME FROM JON'S MOTHER
© 1983 PAWS, INC. All Rights Reserved.

JIM DAVIS
3-9

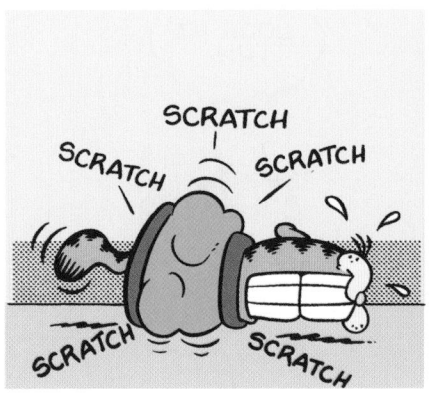
SCRATCH
SCRATCH
SCRATCH
SCRATCH
SCRATCH

I HATE WOOL SWEATERS
© 1983 PAWS, INC. All Rights Reserved.

JIM DAVIS
3-10

THERE IS ONE THING I LIKE ABOUT THIS SWEATER

Z
© 1983 PAWS, INC. All Rights Reserved.

JIM DAVIS
3-11

THERE'S MORE THAN ONE WAY TO SKIN A CAT
TWANG

CHECK THAT... CHOKE A CAT
© 1983 PAWS, INC. All Rights Reserved.

I HATE DESIGNER SWEATERS
JIM DAVIS
3-12

LOOK AT THIS

THE LIZARD CHEWED THE ARMPIT OUT OF IT
© 1983 PAWS, INC. All Rights Reserved.

© 1983 PAWS, INC. All Rights Reserved.

HEY, GARFIELD, LOOK WHAT I GOT AT THE BARBER SHOP
JIM DAVIS
3-14

TAH-DAH! WHAT DO YOU THINK?
IT'S TACKY, TASTELESS AND DISGUSTING

IT'S YOU
© 1983 PAWS, INC. All Rights Reserved.

BINGO!
DOUGHNUTS
JIM DAVIS
3-15

HOOK SHOT
DOUGHNUTS

HA-HA-HA, GARFIELD, HA-HA-HA
DOUGHNUTS
© 1983 PAWS, INC. All Rights Reserved.

JON SURE LOOKS DUMB WITH HIS FAKE MUSTACHE

VERY FEW PEOPLE CAN WEAR A MUSTACHE
JIM DAVIS
3-16

LIKE EVIL ROY GATO, FOR INSTANCE
© 1983 PAWS, INC. All Rights Reserved.

NYAH, NYAH, NYAAAH, EVIL ROY GATO DOES HIS DAILY DIRTY DEED
JIM DAVIS
3-17

PUSH

THE MUSTACHE MADE ME DO IT
© 1983 PAWS, INC. All Rights Reserved.

OH, THERE YOU ARE, GARFIELD
JIM DAVIS
3-18

LET ME GUESS...YOU STOLE MY FAKE MUSTACHE AND ATE MY SPAGHETTI, RIGHT?

HOW'D YOU GUESS?
© 1983 PAWS, INC. All Rights Reserved.

GIVE ME A KISS, SWEETHEART
JIM DAVIS
3-19

KISS

HOW DO YOU TELL A LADY HER MUSTACHE NEEDS MORE WAX?
© 1983 PAWS, INC. All Rights Reserved.

© 1983 PAWS, INC. All Rights Reserved.

Garfield loses his feet

BY JIM DAVIS

Ballantine Books • New York

COME ON, MONDAY! DO IT TO ME NOW! THE SUSPENSE IS KILLING ME!
JIM DAVIS
3-21

THOCK
© 1983 PAWS, INC. All Rights Reserved.

THANK YOU FOR YOUR PROMPT CONSIDERATION

DID I EVER TELL YOU ABOUT MY UNCLE NICK? HE LOVES TO DESTROY THINGS. HE CAN SHRED A RECLINER IN 12 SECONDS...
3-22
JIM DAVIS

MANGLE FERNS BY THE CARLOAD AND TURN A SET OF CHINA INTO POWDER IN THE BLINK OF AN EYE

HE IS PRESENTLY A POSTAL EMPLOYEE IN CHICAGO
© 1983 PAWS, INC. All Rights Reserved.

JIM DAVIS 3-23

NICE TRY, GARFIELD, BUT I DON'T BUY YOUR STUPID WATERMELON DISGUISE
© 1983 PAWS, INC. All Rights Reserved.

RATA TATTA TATTA TATA

JIM DAVIS
3-24

DON'T MAKE FUN OF ODIE, GARFIELD. THAT'S NOT NICE
© 1983 PAWS, INC. All Rights Reserved.

THAT'S EVEN LESS NICE

COME AND GET IT, GARFIELD
GARFIELD
3-25
JIM DAVIS

CRASH!
GARFIELD
© 1983 PAWS, INC. All Rights Reserved.

YOUR NOT A SAILPLANE, YOU KNOW
OH, SHUT UP
GARFIELD

JIM DAVIS
DINNERTIME, GARFIELD!
GARFIELD
3-26

BANZAI
GARFIELD
© 1983 PAWS, INC. All Rights Reserved.

GARFIELD

DO NOT OPEN THIS GATE!
HELLO, WHAT'S THIS?

DO NOT OPEN THIS GATE!
THAT'S AN OPEN INVITATION IF I EVER SAW ONE
© 1983 PAWS, INC. All Rights Reserved.

DO NOT OPEN THIS GATE!
OF COURSE, IT MAY NOT BE WISE TO OPEN THE GATE
JIM DAVIS
3-27

DO NOT OPEN THIS GATE!
BUT THAT NEVER STOPPED ME BEFORE. I'LL JUST TAKE A LITTLE PEEK

CURIOSITY MANGLED THE CAT

PUNT
3-28

THIS IS TURNING OUT TO BE A DECENT MONDAY FOR A CHANGE
© 1983 PAWS, INC. All Rights Reserved.
JIM DAVIS

POOMP!

GOBBLE GOBBLE GOBBLE
GARFIELD
JIM DAVIS
3-29

GARFIELD, YOU EAT TOO FAST
NO, I DON'T
GARFIELD
© 1983 PAWS, INC. All Rights Reserved.

I'M JUST OVERQUALIFIED FOR THE JOB
GARFIELD

GARFIELD WILL NEVER REACH THIS PIE UP HERE
JIM DAVIS 3-30
© 1983 PAWS, INC. All Rights Reserved.

CHINK

AND JUST WHERE ARE YOU GOING?
FOR MY MORNING SCALE?

ARRRRGH!
JIM DAVIS
3-31

WHAT A HORRIBLE NIGHTMARE! I DREAMT I WAS A DOG

THANK GOODNESS IT WAS ONLY A DREAM
SCRATCH SCRATCH SCRATCH
© 1983 PAWS, INC. All Rights Reserved.

NO MORE OF THIS SNIVELING SISSY STUFF
JIM DAVIS
4-1

I'M GETTING OUT OF THIS TREE LIKE A MAN
© 1983 PAWS, INC. All Rights Reserved.

ON THE OTHER HAND, SNIVELING DOES HAVE ITS ATTRIBUTES

I GOTTA GET OUT OF THIS TREE
JIM DAVIS
4-2

OH WELL, THEY TELL ME A CAT ALWAYS LANDS ON HIS FEET

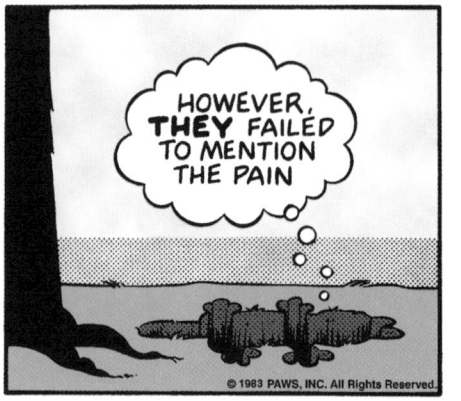
HOWEVER, THEY FAILED TO MENTION THE PAIN
© 1983 PAWS, INC. All Rights Reserved.

GARFIELD®

© 1983 PAWS, INC. All Rights Reserved.

JIM DAVIS
4-3

WE MUST HAVE LUNCH SOMETIME
THINGS AREN'T ALWAYS AS THEY SEEM

HEY, GARFIELD, LET'S TAKE A VACATION
JIM DAVIS
4-4

WE'LL GO SOMEPLACE TROPICAL

SAVE YOUR MONEY. GO SIT IN YOUR AQUARIUM
© 1983 PAWS, INC. All Rights Reserved.

VACATION IS GOING TO BE SO GREAT, GARFIELD
JIM DAVIS
4-5

WE'LL GET AWAY FROM THIS RAT RACE. THERE'LL BE NO HASSLES

A CHANGE OF PACE WOULD BE NICE
© 1983 PAWS, INC. All Rights Reserved.

HEY, GARFIELD, WHAT DO YOU THINK OF THIS SHIRT FOR OUR VACATION?
JIM DAVIS
4-6

TAH-DAH!
THAT'S AWFUL

DO YOU KNOW HOW MANY TURKEYS WERE DESTROYED TO MAKE THAT SHIRT?
© 1983 PAWS, INC. All Rights Reserved.

© 1983 PAWS, INC. All Rights Reserved.

© 1983 PAWS, INC. All Rights Reserved.

© 1983 PAWS, INC. All Rights Reserved.

GARFIELD®

I THINK YOU'LL LIKE FLYING
I'D LIKE IT IF I COULD KEEP ONE PAW ON THE GROUND

© 1983 PAWS, INC. All Rights Reserved.
OOOOOH, I THINK I'M GETTING AIRSICK

WHAT'S THAT? IT SOUNDS LIKE A WING CABLE FRAYING!

I SMELL SMOKE!
SNIFF SNIFF

WE'RE GOING DOWN IN FLAMES!

WE'RE STILL ON THE GROUND, GARFIELD
GREAT! CATS AND CHILDREN FIRST!
JIM DAVIS 4-10

TELL ME, GARFIELD
JIM DAVIS 4-11
ARE YOU NERVOUS ABOUT FLYING?
© 1983 PAWS, INC. All Rights Reserved.
I TAKE NO CHANCES

I THINK YOU'LL ENJOY FLYING, GARFIELD
IT'S A VERY COMFORTABLE AND SMOOTH WAY TO TRAVEL
JIM DAVIS 4-12
THEN WHAT ARE THESE LITTLE BAGS FOR? THE EASTER EGG HUNT?
© 1983 PAWS, INC. All Rights Reserved.

NO PETS ALLOWED
THIS IS MY SON. HE HAS A BODY HAIR PROBLEM
© 1983 PAWS, INC. All Rights Reserved.
JIM DAVIS
HOW OLD ARE YOU, SONNY?
ROWR
4-13
THAT'S BABY TALK FOR "ONE GOING ON TWO"

© 1983 PAWS, INC. All Rights Reserved.

© 1983 PAWS, INC. All Rights Reserved.

© 1983 PAWS, INC. All Rights Reserved.

GARFIELD®

FOR REAL RELAXATION, IT'S HARD TO BEAT THE TROPICS
OH, GO SIT ON A SANDBUR

YOU SHOULD GO PLAY IN THE SURF, GARFIELD
MAYBE NEXT YEAR
© 1983 PAWS, INC. All Rights Reserved.

THERE ARE FISH OUT THERE, YOU KNOW
WELL, WHY DIDN'T YOU SAY SO?!

HA HA HA
JIM DAVIS

SIMPLE CAT, SIMPLE PLEASURES
4-17

DO YOU KNOW WHAT I LOVE ABOUT THE TROPICS, GARFIELD?
I HAVE A FEELING YOU'RE GOING TO TELL ME
JIM DAVIS
4-18

IT'S THE MILES AND MILES OF SPARKLING BEACH

IT MAY BE A BEACH TO YOU, BUT IT'S JUST A SANDBOX TO ME
© 1983 PAWS, INC. All Rights Reserved.

THERE IS ONE THING I LOVE ABOUT THE TROPICS
GRRRR
JIM DAVIS
4-19

FLIP!

THE TINY DOGS
© 1983 PAWS, INC. All Rights Reserved.

YOU DON'T SEEM TO BE HAVING A GOOD TIME, GARFIELD
A KEEN OBSERVATION
4-20

WHAT'S THE PROBLEM?
I TELL YOU WHAT YOU DO
JIM DAVIS
© 1983 PAWS, INC. All Rights Reserved.

FIND THE BIGGEST, HEAVIEST FUR COAT YOU CAN AND PUT IT ON. THEN GO LIE IN THE BLAZING SUN FOR A FEW HOURS AND SEE HOW MANY YUKS YOU HAVE

TELL ME, MY LITTLE WAHINE, WHAT DO YOU DO? I'LL BET YOU WALK ALONG THE BEACH ALL DAY, THEN GO HOME TO YOUR LITTLE THATCHED HUT AT NIGHT, RIGHT?

I'M A COMPUTER PROGRAMMER FROM CLEVELAND

CLOSE. HOW ABOUT A DATE?
HE DIDN'T EVEN BLINK
JIM DAVIS 4-21
© 1983 PAWS, INC. All Rights Reserved.

THIS IS THE LIFE, ISN'T IT, GARFIELD?
MORE FUN THAN A CAT SHOULD HAVE
JIM DAVIS
4-22

NOTHING TO DO BUT LIE HERE IN THE SUN
LISTENING TO YOUR BRAIN BAKE

ARE YOU BORED, GARFIELD?
IS THERE SAND IN YOUR SWIMSUIT?
© 1983 PAWS, INC. All Rights Reserved.

THIS IS GOING TO UPSET YOU, GARFIELD...
JIM DAVIS
4-23

BECAUSE I KNOW YOU'VE HAD A GREAT TIME
© 1983 PAWS, INC. All Rights Reserved.

BUT IT'S TIME WE THINK ABOUT GOING HOME

GARFIELD
THERE'S NOTHING LIKE A BUBBLE BATH TO CURE WHAT AILS YOU, GARFIELD
POP
JIM DAVIS
4-24
POP
POP
© 1983 PAWS, INC. All Rights Reserved.
POW!
HEY, JON. WHAT HAPPENED TO YOU GUYS?
YOU WOULDN'T BELIEVE ME IF I TOLD YOU

Dear Garfield,
What is your favorite all-time film?
4-25
JIM DAVIS

IT'S "OLD YELLER"
© 1983 PAWS, INC. All Rights Reserved.

I LOVE MOVIES WITH HAPPY ENDINGS

JIM DAVIS
4-26

© 1983 PAWS, INC. All Rights Reserved.

AND JUST WHAT DO YOU THINK YOU'RE DOING?
ASSERTING MY CATHOOD?

GARFIELD, WHY IS IT CATS LIKE TO GET OUT AT NIGHT?
4-27
JIM DAVIS

THAT'S WHEN WE LIKE TO SING ON FENCES

IN THE DAYLIGHT, WE'D BE EASY TARGETS
© 1983 PAWS, INC. All Rights Reserved.

TODAY IS THURSDAY, AND THAT'S LASAGNA DAY
JIM DAVIS
4-28

HERE'S YOUR CAT FOOD, GARFIELD. WILL THERE BE ANYTHING ELSE?
GARFIELD

LET ME JOG YOUR MEMORY
© 1983 PAWS, INC. All Rights Reserved.

WHY DO YOU HAVE SUCH LARGE TEETH, GARFIELD?
GARFIELD
JIM DAVIS
4-29

ALL THE BETTER TO EAT YOU WITH, MY DEAR
GARFIELD

STOP THAT!
OBVIOUSLY, SIR, YOU ARE NOT A PATRON OF THE CLASSICS
GARFIELD
© 1983 PAWS, INC. All Rights Reserved.

I SAW AN AWFUL MOVIE LAST NIGHT CALLED "ALIEN DOG." IT WAS ABOUT THIS GIGANTIC MUTT THAT TERRORIZED THE WORLD
JIM DAVIS
4-30

HOWEVER, THEY DID DISPATCH HIM WITH A RATHER CLEVER PLOY

THEY ELECTRIFIED A 12-STORY FIRE HYDRANT
© 1983 PAWS, INC. All Rights Reserved.

GARFIELD®

LET'S PUT THIS WHOLE THING IN PERSPECTIVE
© 1983 PAWS, INC. All Rights Reserved.

EATING IS IMPORTANT
JIM DAVIS
5-1

AND SLEEPING IS IMPORTANT

BUT NOTHING IS MORE IMPORTANT THAN HOLDING SOMEONE YOU LOVE

CHECK THAT

RECIPROCATION IS NICE, TOO

YOU'RE TOO FAT, GARFIELD
HANG IT IN YOUR EAR
JIM DAVIS
5-2

OH, SHUT UP, ODIE

WHY DO I HAVE THE FEELING THERE'S A CONSPIRACY AFOOT?
© 1983 PAWS, INC. All Rights Reserved.

GARFIELD
JIM DAVIS
5-3

ARRRGH!
GARFIELD

IT'S DIET WEEK
IT'S DIET WEEK
© 1983 PAWS, INC. All Rights Reserved.

JIM DAVIS
5-4

I GOTTA GET OFF THIS DIET

IT'S STARTING TO MESS WITH MY MIND
© 1983 PAWS, INC. All Rights Reserved.

JIM DAVIS

5-5
© 1983 PAWS, INC. All Rights Reserved.

RELEASE MY HAND, GARFIELD
YOU RELEASE HAMBURGER, I RELEASE HAND

SUICIDE, EXERCISE AND DIETING
JIM DAVIS
5-6

RIP!

NAME THREE FORMS OF SELF-ABUSE
TRUE... HOW TRUE
© 1983 PAWS, INC. All Rights Reserved.

JIM DAVIS
5-7

© 1983 PAWS, INC. All Rights Reserved.

GARFIELD®

OH, NO! MY WATCH HAS STOPPED!

I'VE MISSED GARFIELD'S MEALTIME

PETS HAVE A WAY OF LETTING YOU KNOW WHEN YOU'VE MISSED THEIR MEALTIME

I KNOW. I KNOW
YOU'RE LATE
JIM DAVIS
5-8
© 1983 PAWS, INC. All Rights Reserved.

TELL ME, GARFIELD, WHEN YOU WALK, DO YOUR RIGHT AND LEFT LEGS TRAVEL TOGETHER, OR DO YOU USE YOUR OPPOSING LEGS ?
JIM DAVIS

© 1983 PAWS, INC. All Rights Reserved.

I'LL NEVER WALK AGAIN
5-9

Z
Z
Z
I WONDER HOW BIRDS CAN SLEEP IN TREES WITHOUT FALLING OUT
JIM DAVIS
5-10

Z
Z
Z

Z
Z
Z
AHA!... HAMMOCKS
© 1983 PAWS, INC. All Rights Reserved.

THIS IS THE ONLY WAY TO SPEND A SUNNY AFTERNOON

ALL YOU NEED IS A SWIMMING POOL

AND A GOOD IMAGINATION
© 1983 PAWS, INC. All Rights Reserved.
JIM DAVIS
5-11

© 1983 PAWS, INC. All Rights Reserved.

© 1983 PAWS, INC. All Rights Reserved.

© 1983 PAWS, INC. All Rights Reserved.

© 1983 PAWS, INC. All Rights Reserved.

HEY, GARFIELD, GUESS WHAT! WE'RE GOING TO VISIT DAD AND MOM ON THE FARM THIS WEEK
5-16
JIM DAVIS

WE'LL EAT SOME OF MOM'S DOWN-HOME COOKING AND HELP DAD WITH THE FARM WORK
© 1983 PAWS, INC. All Rights Reserved.

GOOD THINKING, JON. LET'S DRIVE ALL THE WAY TO THE STICKS AND FETCH US AN APPLE PIE AND A HERNIA

YOUR BROTHER, DOC, HAS COME BACK TO WORK ON THE FARM. HE'S HERE NOW
JIM DAVIS
5-17

DOC BOY!
DON'T CALL ME "DOC BOY"

JON BOY! MOM BOY! DOC BOY! HOW ARE YOU?
OH BOY
© 1983 PAWS, INC. All Rights Reserved.

WHAT BRINGS YOU TO THE FARM, JON?
I PROMISED GARFIELD SOME GOOD HOME COOKING
JIM DAVIS
5-18

WHAT WOULD YOU BOYS LIKE FOR BREAKFAST?

MY GUESS IS GARFIELD WOULD LIKE SOME HAM AND EGGS
© 1983 PAWS, INC. All Rights Reserved.

DOC, YOU'RE LOOKING MORE LIKE DAD ALL THE TIME
JIM DAVIS

YOU TAKE THAT BACK!

© 1983 PAWS, INC. All Rights Reserved.
5-19
SMACK!
HUSH UP, BOY
THE THREE STOOGES LIVE

YOU KNOW, DOC, FOR BROTHERS, WE DON'T LOOK MUCH ALIKE
JIM DAVIS 5-20
© 1983 PAWS, INC. All Rights Reserved.

IT'S HARD TO BELIEVE WE CAME FROM THE SAME PLACE

YOU MEAN, THE FARM?
THE FUNNY FARM MAYBE

TAKE CARE NOW
SEE YOU SOON
DON'T BE A STRANGER
JIM DAVIS

SO LONG!
BYE BYE!
BYE NOW
SEE YUH
© 1983 PAWS, INC. All Rights Reserved.

I CAN'T BELIEVE THE FUSS THEY MAKE OVER GOING TO BED
YOU HAVE A VERY CLOSE FAMILY
5-21

© 1983 PAWS, INC. All Rights Reserved.

© 1983 PAWS, INC. All Rights Reserved.

© 1983 PAWS, INC. All Rights Reserved.

© 1983 PAWS, INC. All Rights Reserved.

© 1983 PAWS, INC. All Rights Reserved.

© 1983 PAWS, INC. All Rights Reserved.

© 1983 PAWS, INC. All Rights Reserved.

© 1983 PAWS, INC. All Rights Reserved.

© 1983 PAWS, INC. All Rights Reserved.

© 1983 PAWS, INC. All Rights Reserved.

GARFIELD®
I WONDER WHAT WOULD HAPPEN IF I MARRIED ARLENE
WE'D HAVE A HUGE WEDDING...
THEN WE'D RAISE SOME KITTENS...
AND THEY'D CRAWL ALL OVER ME
FORGET IT! I'D MAKE A LOUSY FATHER
JIM DAVIS 6-5
© 1983 PAWS, INC. All Rights Reserved.

© 1983 PAWS, INC. All Rights Reserved.

GARFIELD, MEET MY NEW PET FROG, "HERBIE"
JIM DAVIS
6-9

ISN'T HE GREAT?
YEH, GOOD OL' "HERBIE"

GOOD OL' "YOUR DAYS ARE NUMBERED AS SOON AS JON TURNS HIS BACK, HERBIE"
© 1983 PAWS, INC. All Rights Reserved.

ZZZZZZZZ
JIM DAVIS
6-10

HEY, GARFIELD, WHEN WAS THE LAST TIME YOU SAW MY PET FROG, HERBIE?
ZZZ

SNAK!
AT LUNCH
© 1983 PAWS, INC. All Rights Reserved.

IT SEEMS LIKE AN AGE SINCE I GAVE ODIE A BOOT
JIM DAVIS
6-11

BOOT!

I'M JUST A SENTIMENTAL FOOL
© 1983 PAWS, INC. All Rights Reserved.

GARFIELD

HEY, GARFIELD! LET'S HAVE SOME FUN!
FORGET IT, JON

I WANT TO TAKE YOU TO AN ITALIAN RESTAURANT FOR A LASAGNA DINNER
NO WAY
JIM DAVIS
6-12

THEY HAVE FERNS FOR DESSERT
BIG DEAL

THEN WE CAN COME HOME AND I'LL HOLD ODIE DOWN WHILE YOU BEAT HIM UP
TRY AND MAKE ME
© 1983 PAWS, INC. All Rights Reserved.

HOW DID YOU KNOW WE HAVE AN APPOINTMENT AT THE VET'S?
I DON'T KNOW. I JUST KNOW

© 1983 PAWS, INC. All Rights Reserved.

JIM DAVIS
6-16

MOTHER NATURE HAS CERTAINLY BEEN KIND TO YOU, GARFIELD

I WISH I COULD SAY THE SAME FOR FATHER TIME
© 1983 PAWS, INC. All Rights Reserved.

THEY SAY THE FIRST THING TO GO ON A CAT IS ITS HEARING
JIM DAVIS
6-17

OR WAS THAT EYESIGHT?
© 1983 PAWS, INC. All Rights Reserved.

YOUR BIRTHDAY GIFT IS INSIDE THIS CARD, GARFIELD
JIM DAVIS 6-18

SOMEDAY, MY SIGNATURE WILL BE WORTH A LOT OF MONEY!

© 1983 PAWS, INC. All Rights Reserved.

©1983 PAWS, INC. All Rights Reserved.

© 1983 PAWS, INC. All Rights Reserved.

© 1983 PAWS, INC. All Rights Reserved.

© 1983 PAWS, INC. All Rights Reserved.

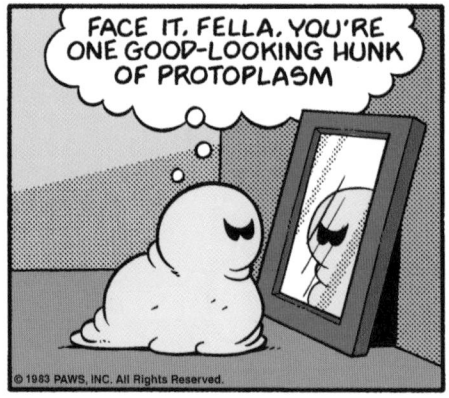

© 1983 PAWS, INC. All Rights Reserved.

© 1983 PAWS, INC. All Rights Reserved.

© 1983 PAWS, INC. All Rights Reserved.

© 1983 PAWS, INC. All Rights Reserved.

© 1983 PAWS, INC. All Rights Reserved.

© 1983 PAWS, INC. All Rights Reserved.

COOKIES
JIM DAVIS
6-30

COOKIES

COOKIE
© 1983 PAWS, INC. All Rights Reserved.

GARFIELD! YOU ATE MY RAISIN COOKIES!
COOKIES
JIM DAVIS
7-1

I THOUGHT YOU DIDN'T LIKE RAISINS
COOKIES

I DON'T
COOKIES
© 1983 PAWS, INC. All Rights Reserved.

SHOO! SHOO! .GO AWAY! I DON'T LIKE YOU
JIM DAVIS
7-2

SLURP!

I HATE BLIND DEVOTION
© 1983 PAWS, INC. All Rights Reserved.

© 1983 PAWS, INC. All Rights Reserved.

GARFIELD, I KNOW YOU'RE IN MY FERN. I CAN SEE YOUR TAIL
JIM DAVIS
7-4

WHAT DO YOU HAVE TO SAY FOR YOURSELF?
© 1983 PAWS, INC. All Rights Reserved.

I SAY WE ATTACK THE FORT AT DAWN

I WONDER WHAT THIS IS
JIM DAVIS
7-5

© 1983 PAWS, INC. All Rights Reserved.

AH, A BOOBY TRAP

JIM DAVIS

© 1983 PAWS, INC. All Rights Reserved.
7-6

© 1983 PAWS, INC. All Rights Reserved.

© 1983 PAWS, INC. All Rights Reserved.

© 1983 PAWS, INC. All Rights Reserved.

GARFIELD®

WHAT DO YOU THINK OF MY MING VASE, GARFIELD?

CRASH!

MING, SHMING. THEY DON'T MAKE'M LIKE THEY USED TO

WHA!... GUH!... I DON'T!... BUH!... YOU!... YOU!

YOU DUMB ANIMAL! YOU'RE SO STUPID, YOU DON'T KNOW WHAT YOU DID
© 1983 PAWS, INC. All Rights Reserved.

I KNOW I DESTROYED A PRICELESS MING DYNASTY VASE AS AN OVERT EXPRESSION TO COMMUNICATE MY CONTEMPT FOR THE POLITICALLY OPPRESSIVE DOCTRINES OF THEIR EARLY 17TH CENTURY ADMINISTRATION
JIM DAVIS 7-10

I COULD SURE USE SOME OF JON'S DEODORANT
JIM DAVIS 7-11

SSST

HOW'S IT GOING, GARFIELD?
FINE, UNTIL I FOUND THE SPRAY STARCH IN YOUR CABINET
© 1983 PAWS, INC. All Rights Reserved.

GO FETCH THE PAPER, WILL YOU, GARFIELD?
THAT'S WHAT I LIVE FOR

JIM DAVIS 7-12
HERE YOU ARE, SAHIB
© 1983 PAWS, INC. All Rights Reserved.

HEY! THIS PAPER IS ALL CHEWED UP!
SAHIB ASKS FISH, PAPER IS WET. SAHIB ASKS CAT, PAPER IS HOLEY

JIM DAVIS
7-13

WAH-HA HA-HA!
I HATE IT WHEN THEY DO THAT
© 1983 PAWS, INC. All Rights Reserved.

WATER
JIM DAVIS
7-14

SLUP SLUP SLUP
WATER
© 1983 PAWS, INC. All Rights Reserved.

DROOL FUEL
WATER

AW... HOW SWEET
7-15
JIM DAVIS

WAIT A MINUTE! I'LL BET YOU WANT SOMETHING FROM ME, DON'T YOU?
© 1983 PAWS, INC. All Rights Reserved.

HOW DARE YOU SUGGEST I TRADE MY AFFECTION FOR SELFISH REASONS! FOR A BITE OF THAT HAMBURGER, I'LL FORGET YOU SAID THAT

GARFIELD, I KNOW YOU'RE IN MY FERN. I CAN SEE YOUR TAIL

WHAT DO YOU HAVE TO SAY FOR YOURSELF?
© 1983 PAWS, INC. All Rights Reserved.

ARF?
JIM DAVIS
7-16

GARFIELD®
I AM ABOUT TO OUTDO MYSELF
7-17
JIM DAVIS
WHAP!
©1983 PAWS, INC. All Rights Reserved.

GARFIELD, I KNOW YOU'RE IN MY FERN. I CAN SEE YOUR TAIL

WHAT DO YOU HAVE TO SAY FOR YOURSELF?
© 1983 PAWS, INC. All Rights Reserved.

PARDON ME, SIR. HAVE YOU SEEN A TAIL AROUND HERE?
JIM DAVIS
7-18

YOU DON'T LIKE ME, DO YOU?
I LIKE YOU
JIM DAVIS

NO, YOU DON'T
I'M CRAZY ABOUT YOU. I LOVE YOU
7-19

NOW WHY DON'T YOU GO PLAY IN THE BLENDER?
SEE?
© 1983 PAWS, INC. All Rights Reserved.

WHY DON'T YOU LIKE ME?
YOU'RE YOUNG AND YOU'RE CUTE
JIM DAVIS
7-20

IF I WERE OLD AND UGLY, WOULD YOU LIKE ME?
POSSIBLY

THIS MUST BE ONE OF THE THINGS CATS DO WHEN THEY THINK THERE ARE NO HUMANS AROUND
WHERE'S MY CANE? WHERE'S MY CANE?
© 1983 PAWS, INC. All Rights Reserved.

© 1983 PAWS, INC. All Rights Reserved.

GARFIELD

RISE AND SHINE

TIME TO GET UP, JON

I'M HUNGRY

THIS OUGHT TO WAKE HIM UP

JIM DAVIS
7-24
JON MUST REALLY BE SOCKED OUT
© 1983 PAWS, INC. All Rights Reserved.

I WASN'T ABOUT TO GIVE HIM THE SATISFACTION

GARFIELD, I KNOW YOU'RE IN MY FERN. I CAN SEE YOUR TAIL

WHAT DO YOU HAVE TO SAY FOR YOURSELF ?
© 1983 PAWS, INC. All Rights Reserved.

YOU'LL HAVE TO SPEAK UP. I CAN'T HEAR YOU OVER THE BAND
JIM DAVIS
7-25

JIM DAVIS
7-26

GEE... UH, THANKS, ODIE
CLUNK!

WHAT IS IT, GARFIELD?
I'D WAGER IT WOULD HAVE BEEN EASIER TO RECOGNIZE BEFORE IT WANDERED INTO TRAFFIC
© 1983 PAWS, INC. All Rights Reserved.

HERE COMES ODIE. HIS BARK IS WORSE THAN HIS BITE
BARK! BARK!

© 1983 PAWS, INC. All Rights Reserved.
BARK!

AND HIS BREATH IS WORSE THAN HIS BARK
JIM DAVIS 7-27

© 1983 PAWS, INC. All Rights Reserved.

© 1983 PAWS, INC. All Rights Reserved.

© 1983 PAWS, INC. All Rights Reserved.

RRR
JIM DAVIS
8-4

RRR!!!!!

I WANT TO KNOW WHY YOU DID THAT, GARFIELD!
THAT'S NOT HALF AS INTERESTING AS HOW I GOT UP THERE TO BEGIN WITH
© 1983 PAWS, INC. All Rights Reserved.

GARFIELD, I WANT YOU TO GET ALL THE MICE OUT OF THIS HOUSE, RIGHT NOW!
OH, VERY WELL
JIM DAVIS
8-5

BE A GOOD BOY AND CALL MY ATTORNEY, WILL YOU?

AND HAVE HIM SERVE THEM WITH AN EVICTION NOTICE
© 1983 PAWS, INC. All Rights Reserved.

JIM DAVIS
8-6

ARRRGH!!!
B-B-B-B!

CATS ARE SO UNPREDICTABLE
PREDICTABLY SO
© 1983 PAWS, INC. All Rights Reserved.

GARFIELD®

GARFIELD, WHY DON'T YOU EAT MICE LIKE OTHER CATS?
I DON'T LIKE TO HURT MICE. HOW CAN I GET THAT THROUGH YOUR THICK SKULL?

Dear Jon: The mice and I have an agreement. They don't bug me and I don't bug them. Therefore, I will never hurt mice...signed,
GARFI*
TICK
TICK
TICK
JIM DAVIS
8-7

GARFI**********
THE KEY MUST BE STUCK
TICK!
TICK!
TICK!

AAAWK!
WHAM
© 1983 PAWS, INC. All Rights Reserved.

SORRY ABOUT THAT, FELLA

GARFIELD
JIM DAVIS
8-8

OH, NO!
GARFIELD
© 1983 PAWS, INC. All Rights Reserved.

MY LEGS ARE SHRINKING!
GARFIELD

I'VE REALLY DONE IT THIS TIME. MY BELLY HAS OUTGROWN MY LEGS
JIM DAVIS
8-9

I GUESS THERE'S ONLY ONE THING TO DO...

GET FITTED FOR STILTS
© 1983 PAWS, INC. All Rights Reserved.

♪ HUMMM ♫
JIM DAVIS
8-10

OH, NO!

YOU KNOW YOU'RE OVERWEIGHT WHEN YOU'RE SITTING AROUND ROCKING, AND YOU REALIZE YOU DON'T HAVE A ROCKING CHAIR
© 1983 PAWS, INC. All Rights Reserved.

GARFIELD, YOU'RE GETTING DANGEROUSLY OVERWEIGHT
WATER
8-11
JIM DAVIS

HOW DANGEROUS CAN A LITTLE EXTRA FAT BE?
WATER

WHO, BLUB, WOULD, BLUB, HAVE, BLUB, GUESSED?
WATER
© 1983 PAWS, INC. All Rights Reserved.

DON'T WORRY ABOUT YOUR CONDITION, GARFIELD
JIM DAVIS
8-12

YOU CAN STILL LEAD A USEFUL AND PRODUCTIVE LIFE

AS A PAPERWEIGHT, A DOORSTOP, A...
PUT YOUR FACE CLOSER TO THESE CLAWS
© 1983 PAWS, INC. All Rights Reserved.

RATS! IT'S THE DOG NEXT DOOR!
JIM DAVIS
8-13

© 1983 PAWS, INC. All Rights Reserved.

EVER HAD A NIGHTMARE COME TRUE?

GARFIELD

HI, HI, DAISY-WAISY. WOULD YOU WIKE SOME WA-WA?
OH BOYSY-WOYSY

IF YOU SPEAK NICELY TO PLANTS, THEY GROW BETTER, GARFIELD
BOLOGNA
JIM DAVIS

© 1983 PAWS, INC. All Rights Reserved.
8-14

DIE!

LIVE AND LEARN

JIM DAVIS 8-15

RIIIP!

CRUELTY IS SECOND NATURE TO THAT CAT
© 1983 PAWS, INC. All Rights Reserved.

JIM DAVIS 8-16

DIET TIME
RATS
© 1983 PAWS, INC. All Rights Reserved.

HAPPY DIET, GARFIELD. HERE'S A BANANA FOR BREAKFAST
8-17
JIM DAVIS

BANG!
© 1983 PAWS, INC. All Rights Reserved.

© 1983 PAWS, INC. All Rights Reserved.

© 1983 PAWS, INC. All Rights Reserved.

GARFIELD®
JIM DAVIS 8-21
© 1983 PAWS, INC. All Rights Reserved.
THEY SAY WE CAN VISIT HIM 2 TO 4 ON SATURDAYS
FOOD GONE! FOOD ALL GONE!

© 1983 PAWS, INC. All Rights Reserved.

© 1983 PAWS, INC. All Rights Reserved.

© 1983 PAWS, INC. All Rights Reserved.

© 1983 PAWS, INC. All Rights Reserved.

© 1983 PAWS, INC. All Rights Reserved.

© 1983 PAWS, INC. All Rights Reserved.

GARFIELD

SPLUT
GARFIE

PLIK

BAT
© 1983 PAWS, INC. All Rights Reserved.

SCRATCH
JIM DAVIS

DRIP
WATER
8-28

BORED, GARFIELD?
SOME DAYS I GET TIRED OF BEING A CAT
WATER

© 1983 PAWS, INC. All Rights Reserved.

© 1983 PAWS, INC. All Rights Reserved.

© 1983 PAWS, INC. All Rights Reserved.

© 1983 PAWS, INC. All Rights Reserved.

GARFIELD®

IT'S TIME YOU BOYS LEARN WHERE THE FIRE EXIT IS

IN CASE OF FIRE, GO STRAIGHT TO YOUR SWINGING PET DOOR. GOT THAT?

I'D BETTER GIVE THEM A LITTLE TEST
JIM DAVIS
9-4

FIRE!
© 1983 PAWS, INC. All Rights Reserved.

CLEVER ME

JON MUST BE CLEANING THE HEATING GRATE. I WONDER WHAT GRATES ARE FOR, ANYWAY
JIM DAVIS
9-5

OOPS!
© 1983 PAWS, INC. All Rights Reserved.

OBVIOUSLY, THEY'RE TO KEEP ONE'S HOUSE FROM EATING ONE'S CAT

SILLY ME HAD TO FALL INTO THE HEATING VENT. NOW HERE I AM, RESIDING DEEP WITHIN THE BOWELS OF MY HOME
JIM DAVIS
9-6

FORCED TO SPEND MY REMAINING DAYS FENDING FOR MYSELF IN THE TIN TUNNELS OF THE DUCT WORK, THE SOLENOID JUNGLE OF THE WIRING SYSTEM AND THE POLYVINYL CHLORIDE PLAYGROUND IN THE CRAWL SPACE
© 1983 PAWS, INC. All Rights Reserved.

HEY! I THINK THERE'S A BOOK HERE SOMEWHERE

JIM DAVIS
MEYOW!
9-7

GARFIELD! WHERE ARE YOU?
I'M IN THE PLUMBING

WHAT CAN I DO?
JUST DON'T FLUSH THE TOILET
© 1983 PAWS, INC. All Rights Reserved.

© 1983 PAWS, INC. All Rights Reserved.

© 1983 PAWS, INC. All Rights Reserved.

© 1983 PAWS, INC. All Rights Reserved.

© 1983 PAWS, INC. All Rights Reserved.

© 1983 PAWS, INC. All Rights Reserved.

© 1983 PAWS, INC. All Rights Reserved.

© 1983 PAWS, INC. All Rights Reserved.

© 1983 PAWS, INC. All Rights Reserved.

© 1983 PAWS, INC. All Rights Reserved.

© 1983 PAWS, INC. All Rights Reserved.

GARFIELD®

IF YOU EAT THIS PIE, I'M GOING TO KILL YOU

© 1983 PAWS, INC. All Rights Reserved.

GARFIELD! YOU ATE MY PIE!
JIM DAVIS
9-18

ONE OF THE GREAT CRIMINAL MINDS OF OUR TIME, I AIN'T

© 1983 PAWS, INC. All Rights Reserved.

© 1983 PAWS, INC. All Rights Reserved.

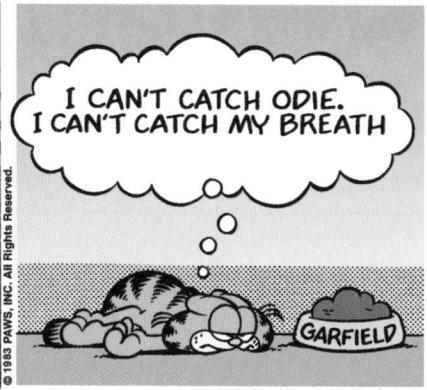

© 1983 PAWS, INC. All Rights Reserved.

© 1983 PAWS, INC. All Rights Reserved.

© 1983 PAWS, INC. All Rights Reserved.

© 1983 PAWS, INC. All Rights Reserved.

GARFIELD®

THIS SIDEWALK IS ALREADY HOT

OOCH! EECH! OUCH!
© 1983 PAWS, INC. All Rights Reserved.

OOG! ARGG! ICK!
JIM DAVIS
9-25

GARFIELD! WHAT ARE YOU DOING ON THIS HOT SIDEWALK?

WHY DON'T WE GO INSIDE?

WHAT? AND DISAPPOINT MY PUBLIC?
CLINK

I'M NOT ONE TO BRAG ON MY TEDDY BEAR, BUT YOU ARE NOT GOING TO BELIEVE THIS
JIM DAVIS

OKAY, POOKY, PAY ATTENTION NOW. ARE YOU READY?
© 1983 PAWS, INC. All Rights Reserved.
9-26

PLAY DEAD!

I'M GETTING TOO OLD TO HAVE A TEDDY BEAR
9-27
JIM DAVIS

IT'S NOT THAT I FEEL SILLY...

IT'S THE PEER PRESSURE
© 1983 PAWS, INC. All Rights Reserved.

POOKY, I HAVE TO START WEANING MYSELF FROM YOU. I GOTTA MAKE IT OUT THERE ON MY OWN
JIM DAVIS
9-28

THAT'S GOOD ENOUGH FOR THE FIRST WEEK
© 1983 PAWS, INC. All Rights Reserved.

© 1983 PAWS, INC. All Rights Reserved.

© 1983 PAWS, INC. All Rights Reserved.

© 1983 PAWS, INC. All Rights Reserved.

© 1983 PAWS, INC. All Rights Reserved.

© 1983 PAWS, INC. All Rights Reserved.

© 1983 PAWS, INC. All Rights Reserved.

© 1983 PAWS, INC. All Rights Reserved.

© 1983 PAWS, INC. All Rights Reserved.

© 1983 PAWS, INC. All Rights Reserved.

GARFIELD

I WISH I COULD KICK THIS INDUSTRIAL-STRENGTH DEPRESSION I HAVE TODAY

JIM DAVIS
10-9

MOTHER NATURE, IF YOU HAD A BODY AND A FACE, I'D GIVE YOU A HUG AND A KISS
© 1983 PAWS, INC. All Rights Reserved.

HERE COMES ARLENE. SHE'S CRAZY ABOUT ME
JIM DAVIS
10-10

HI, ARLENE
© 1983 PAWS, INC. All Rights Reserved.

I SAID... "HI, ARLENE"

HEY, ARLENE. GUESS HOW MUCH WEIGHT I CAN PRESS
JIM DAVIS
10-11

I'LL BET YOU DON'T KNOW
I'LL BET I DON'T CARE
© 1983 PAWS, INC. All Rights Reserved.

RIGHT NOW I'D TRADE ALL THIS STRENGTH FOR JUST ONE SNAPPY COMEBACK

HEY, ARLENE. LOOK AT THIS
SO WHAT?
JIM DAVIS
10-12

JUST WHAT DOES IT TAKE TO IMPRESS YOU, LADY?
A CHALLENGE TO MY HEAD AS WELL AS MY HEART
© 1983 PAWS, INC. All Rights Reserved.

AS SOON AS SHE REGAINS CONSCIOUSNESS, I'LL CHALLENGE THE HEART PART

© 1983 PAWS, INC. All Rights Reserved.

© 1983 PAWS, INC. All Rights Reserved.

© 1983 PAWS, INC. All Rights Reserved.

GARFIELD

ODIE, ALL YOU EVER DO IS STARE AND SLOBBER

YOU'RE TOO HAPPY, AND THAT'S NOT HEALTHY
JIM DAVIS
10-16

PEOPLE DON'T TRUST A CHRONICALLY HAPPY PERSON
© 1983 PAWS, INC. All Rights Reserved.

WHO COULD POSSIBLY LOVE A GRINNING IDIOT LIKE YOU?

YOU STAY OUT OF THIS

© 1983 PAWS, INC. All Rights Reserved.

© 1983 PAWS, INC. All Rights Reserved.

© 1983 PAWS, INC. All Rights Reserved.

WHY ARE WE SO DEPRESSED, GARFIELD?
I HAVE THIS THEORY
JIM DAVIS
10-20
© 1983 PAWS, INC. All Rights Reserved.
WE'VE BEEN STAYING UP TOO LATE, LATELY
AND BEING HAPPY TAKES ENTIRELY TOO MUCH ENERGY

WE'VE GOTTA DO SOMETHING ABOUT THIS DEPRESSION, GARFIELD
CHECK
JIM DAVIS
10-21
© 1983 PAWS, INC. All Rights Reserved.
MAYBE A CHANGE OF SURROUNDINGS WOULD CHEER US UP
CHECK
WRONGO
CHECK

THERE'S ONLY ONE WAY OUT OF THIS DEEP BLUE FUNK WE'RE IN, GARFIELD. I HATE TO DO IT, BUT IT HAS TO BE DONE
I HOPE IT WORKS
JIM DAVIS
10-22
© 1983 PAWS, INC. All Rights Reserved.
OOCH! EECH!
TAH-DAH!
BINGO!

GARFIELD®
HEY!
CLICK
I WAS WATCHING "CHEERLEADER HIGH"
CLICK
WELL, I'M WATCHING "WONDER CAT"!
CLICK
JIM DAVIS
RIP
CRASH
© 1983 PAWS, INC. All Rights Reserved.
I WAS MUCH MORE PASSIVE BEFORE I BECAME A WONDER CAT CADET
10-23

I'VE OFTEN WONDERED WHAT I COULD DO IF I WEREN'T ENTERTAINING YOU. HERE ARE JUST A FEW OF THE POSSIBILITIES!
SHORT-ORDER COOK
DOG CATCHER
MATTRESS TESTER
Z
TESTER
PET-STORE OWNER

GARFIELD CHARACTERS THAT DIDN'T MAKE IT

When I initially designed GARFIELD, these concepts never made it off the drawing board. Maybe they could all be brought back in a strip called ROGUES' GALLERY.

JIM DAVIS